Why Do Christians Suffer?

by Theodore H. Epp

A
BACK TO THE BIBLE
PUBLICATION

D1019415

Back to the Bible

Lincoln, Nebraska 68501

231,000 printed to date—1978
(5-7592—70M—88)
ISBN 0-8474-0731-4

Printed in the United States of America

Foreword

This book will be helpful to those who are suffering as well as to those who may not now be passing through any particular trial. It will encourage those who are presently suffering, and it will prepare those who are not now suffering—but who may soon be passing through a severe test.

This book sets forth what the Bible has to say about suffering. Only in the Bible do we find the solution to the mystery of suffering. Only here can believers find how they can have joy, assurance of salvation, and the right attitude while passing through severe trials.

Those who are wondering why they are suffering, and want to know how to have victory in the midst of suffering, will find special help in the pages of this book. When the purpose of suffering is understood, it results in a right attitude toward suffering. There are many practical suggestions in this book which will be of great help in times of suffering.

The "thought" which appears at the end of each chapter has been taken from *The Cream Book*, compiled by Keith L. Brooks, and is used by permission.

—The Publishers

Contents

Contents

Chapter 1

Suffering Is a Mystery

Are you discouraged because of suffering? Job said, "Man is born unto trouble, as the sparks fly upward" (Job 5:7). Through this and other verses, the Word of God tells us that we live in a world of suffering. Job also said, "Man that is born of a woman is of few days, and full of trouble" (Job 14:1). In Ecclesiastes 2:22,23 King Solomon declared, "For what hath man of all his labour, and of the vexation of his heart, wherein he hath laboured under the sun? For all his days are sorrows, and his travail grief; yea, his heart taketh not rest in the night. This is also vanity."

These words emphasize the mystery of suffering. The question that perplexes Christians of the 20th century is the same question that perplexed believers centuries before Christ: Why do Christians suffer?

In seeking the cause of suffering, we need to go back to the book of beginnings—the Book of Genesis. There we find that suffering has resulted from a system of evil. Notice what God said to Adam and Eve after they had fallen into sin: "Unto the woman he said, I will greatly multiply thy sorrow and thy conception; in sorrow thou shalt bring forth children; and thy desire shall be to thy husband, and he shall rule over thee. And unto Adam he said, Because thou hast hearkened unto the voice of thy wife, and hast eaten of the tree, of which I commanded thee, saying, Thou shalt not eat of it: cursed is the ground for thy sake; in sorrow shalt thou eat of it all the days of thy life; Thorns also and thistles shall it bring forth to thee; and thou shalt eat the herb of the field; In the sweat of thy face shalt thou eat bread, till thou return unto the ground; for out of it wast thou taken: for dust thou art, and unto dust shalt thou return" (Gen. 3:16-19).

Notice the occurrences of the word "sorrow" in this passage. God told the woman, "I will greatly multiply thy sorrow and thy conception; in sorrow thou shalt bring forth children." God told Adam, "Cursed is the ground for thy sake; in sorrow shalt thou eat of it all the days of thy life." Thus we see that suffering and sorrow are the result of sin. If there had been no sin, there would be no suffering. We do not suffer to pay the penalty for sin—Christ did this when He died on the cross. The Christian suffers so that God's image—lost because of the Fall—might be restored in him. This is why "all things work together for good to them that love God, to them who are the called according to his purpose" (Rom. 8:28).

Many ask if there will ever be an end to suffering. First Peter 1:7 (a verse which every Christian should memorize) refers to the end of suffering. It says that the reason for the manifold temptations is "that the trial of your faith, being much more precious than of gold that perisheth, though it be tried with fire, might be found unto praise and honour and glory at the appearing of Jesus Christ."

Could God Have Spared Us?

The Lord Jesus Christ warned Christians they would experience suffering in this world. He said, "In the world ye shall have tribulation: but be of good cheer; I have overcome the world" (John 16:33). In the mystery of suffering there remains the question, Could not God have spared man from all this suffering? Because we know God is omnipotent, most of us would agree that He could have saved us from suffering if He had wanted to. Perhaps you ask, If this is true, why did He not spare us? The more we seek for answers, the more we become convinced that suffering is a mystery.

However, there is another aspect that we should consider. If God could have spared us from suffering in the first place, can He not spare us from this suffering now? The answer is obviously Yes. But again comes the question, Then why doesn't He do it? And the mystery of suffering continues.

Those who experience and observe suffering often keep asking, Why? Why? Why? Not only do people suffer, but animal and plant life also suffer. When man sees all of this suffering about him he continues to ask why?

Man's life begins with travail—the travail of a mother. This is the fulfillment of God's words to the woman that her sorrow and conception would be multiplied (Gen. 3:16). Man's life begins with sorrow and it ends with sorrow. Man's experience verifies the words of Job 14:1: "Man that is born

9

of a woman is of few days, and full of trouble." Even after a person is gone from this life there is sorrowing by his friends who dearly miss him. Sorrow is everywhere.

Eyes were created to see, but some are blind. Ears were created to hear, but some are deaf. Hands were made to work, but disease renders them limp and useless. Lungs were made to breathe, but they become cancerous and bring an end to breathing. Brains were made to think, but some suffer brain damage. Suffering is all around us.

Not only is there physical anguish, but there is mental anguish as well. Hopes and dreams of a lifetime are dashed to the ground. Close friends betray us in times of crisis. A life companion is found to be disloyal. A son or a daughter brings disgrace to the home. Sin enters when we are caught off-guard and for the rest of our lives there seems to be remorse. Why? Why this dark mystery of suffering? Is there no God? Does He not care? Is there no relief? Why? Why this prolonged struggle and vale of tears? Why? Is there no answer? Yes, there is an answer. The mystery of suffering is not a mystery that need remain if we search the Word of God.

Job's Example

The Book of Job is a key book of the Bible regarding suffering. Although the entire book deals with this subject, the first two chapters are especially important to the understanding of the whole book. In the first chapter we are told, "The Lord said unto Satan, Hast thou considered my servant Job, that there is none like him in the earth, a perfect and an upright man, one that feareth God, and escheweth evil" (v. 8). What a statement by God! The same statement is repeated in verse 3 of the second chapter where God adds the words: "And still he holdeth fast his integrity, although thou movedst me against him, to destroy him without cause." Job was a good man; God Himself said this was so. But in two successive strokes, Job was stripped of all his possessions, his family and his health. Disease, distress and loathsomeness entered his life. His friends thought such suffering could only come because of sin so they urged Job to confess his sin. With all the world's wisdom they accused him but they had nothing to offer him. One wonders what present-day psychologists and psychiatrists—men filled with this world's wisdom—would have said to Job. Most would have little to offer to Job in explaining why he was suffering. Job had lost everything but he was a godly, righteous man. We know this because God said so. But Job's suffering and the accusations from his friends drove him to self-justification. At first this defeated God's purpose for the suffering.

Job was not able to see the full picture as we now see it. For us, the Book of Job takes up the scene behind the scene—it gives us God's answer to the question, Why do Christians suffer?

Satan, the accuser of the brethren, came into the presence of God. After God told Satan what a godly man Job was, Satan said in effect, "No wonder! The only reason Job has been fearing You is because You have been pampering him; You have put a hedge around him so nothing can happen to him. Take away his house and all his possessions and he will curse You to Your face." To show Satan he was wrong, God said in effect, "All right, go do it." Satan took everything away from Job but Job kept his integrity. The last verse of chapter 1 is a divine commentary on Job's experience: "In all this Job sinned not, nor charged God foolishly" (v. 22).

When Satan came before God again, God said, "See, Job remained faithful." "Yes," replied Satan, "but the most important thing to man is his health. Take away his health and you will see that Job will curse You to Your face." So God permitted Satan to take away Job's health. The rest of the book records Job's physical suffering.

Why did God permit Job to suffer? First, it was God's way of proving Satan was a liar. Second, God was vindicated in Job's trial. Third, it allowed Job to demonstrate his continuous loyalty to God. This loyalty is seen in its epitomy when Job cried out, "Though he slay me, yet will I trust in him" (13:15).

When the suffering was over, Job emerged a better man. Even during his suffering, Job knew this would be true for he said, "When he hath tried me, I shall come forth as gold" (23:10). The end result of Job's suffering is seen in his own testimony: "I have heard of thee by the hearing of the ear: but now mine eye seeth thee. Wherefore I abhor myself, and repent in dust and ashes" (42:5,6).

In Job's experience we are given the master key in understanding the purpose of suffering. As a result of his suffering he received a new revelation of God—"Now mine eye seeth thee."

Seeing God in all His holiness and glory made a completely different man out of Job even though he was already good, according to the testimony of God. As a result of Job's new understanding of God, he said, "I abhor myself." And those of us who have such little suffering in comparison to Christ's suffering should also abhor ourselves instead of complaining so much about it.

Job's Blessing

The last chapter of the Book of Job tells us what followed Job's suffering. In verse 12 we are told, "So the Lord blessed the latter end of Job more than his beginning." This verse has a special message for us regarding suffering. It emphasizes much the same truth as Hebrews 12:11 which tells us that "no chastening for the present seemeth to be joyous, but grievous: nevertheless afterward it yieldeth the peaceable fruit of righteousness unto them which are exercised thereby." Notice especially the word "afterward" in this verse. This is a word that needs to become a permanent part of your vocabulary as far as testing is concerned. Every time you feel the urge to quarrel with God or charge Him falsely for the way He has dealt with you, this word should be remembered. "Afterward"—after the chastening is past—it "yieldeth the peaceable fruit of righteousness unto them which are exercised thereby." It is through this kind of suffering that we really learn to know Christ.

The Apostle Paul knew the blessing of suffering and he expressed his great desire in Philippians 3:10: "That I may know him, and the power of his resurrection, and the fellowship of his sufferings, being made conformable unto his death." Jesus Christ was so precious to the Apostle Paul that he wanted to know all of this.

Thought: Do you believe in the sun when it is hidden behind the clouds? Then doubt not the goodness of God when He seems to hide His face.

Chapter 2

The Basic Cause of Suffering

Although different circumstances bring about suffering, it is important that we know what is the basic cause of suffering. I am referring to that which causes suffering not only to man but also to God.

After the serpent tempted Adam and Eve and they had fallen into sin, God said to the serpent, "Because thou hast done this, thou art cursed . . . ." (Gen. 3:14). The basic cause of suffering is seen in the phrase "because thou hast done this." This same phrase could have been used concerning the woman—"Because thou hast done this, I will greatly multiply thy sorrow and thy conception." This phrase could also have been used for Adam—"Because thou hast done this, cursed is the ground for thy sake; in sorrow shalt thou eat of it all the days of thy life."

Perhaps you say, "But that was Adam and Eve. Why has that anything to do with my suffering?" It has to do with your suffering because it was with Adam and Eve that all suffering originated. Why does suffering exist today? It is because of sin. Adam and Eve sinned and brought sin and suffering on the entire human race. Romans 5:12

15

tells us, "Wherefore, as by one man sin entered into the world, and death by sin; and so death passed upon all men, for that all have sinned."

The Book of Genesis is the book of beginnings or origins. It tells us the origin of the world, man, animal and plant life. It also tells us of the origin of sin which resulted in suffering and separation from God. This explains why things are as they are instead of as they should be. Later on in His Book, God tells how things should be, but the first three chapters tell us why things are as they are. Genesis tells us of the beginnings of sin, sorrow and suffering—the origin of our separation from God.

Created in the Image of God

Man was made in the image of God. Genesis 1:26,27 tells us, "And God said, Let us make man in our image, after our likeness: and let them have dominion over the fish of the sea, and over the fowl of the air, and over the cattle, and over all the earth, and over every creeping thing that creepeth upon the earth. So God created man in his own image, in the image of God created he him; male and female created he them." This does not mean that man was created in the image of God as far as his physical shape is concerned. This would be impossible because God is spirit. But God made man like Himself. He reproduced Himself. He did not produce gods, but He reproduced a spiritual aspect of Himself in man. In other words, He created man in such a way that man would answer only to Him. Man was to have fellowship and enjoyment with God and was to be responsible

16

only to God. What a wonderful purpose God had for man!

After God made man, He also made woman. Genesis 2:21,22 tells us that "the Lord God caused a deep sleep to fall upon Adam, and he slept: and he took one of his ribs, and closed up the flesh instead thereof; And the rib, which the Lord God had taken from man, made he a woman, and brought her unto the man." The woman was made from man and, as such, she was to answer to man. God had made woman for man so that man could have fellowship with one of his own kind. When the woman was made from Adam's rib, Adam said, "This is now bone of my bones, and flesh of my flesh: she shall be called Woman, because she was taken out of Man" (Gen. 2:23). The two were to have fellowship with each other and fellowship with God. God placed them in the Garden of Eden with every provision they needed. They were shut in to God Himself in the Garden. They had perfect love for each other and for God, and of course God's love was perfect for them. Adam and Eve had perfect joy and harmony—no sorrow, no suffering, nothing to annoy, nothing to disappoint them. There were perfect conditions and perfect relationships—no tears and no occasion for suffering. None of these tragic things existed then because God had made man for Himself and woman for man. Together they had wonderful fellowship.

Satan Drives a Wedge

Satan was not about to let this relationship continue if he could help it. He appeared to Eve as

17

a serpent, and we are told in Genesis 3:1 that "the serpent was more subtil than any beast of the field which the Lord God had made." Satan came on the scene in Genesis, even as he is described in II Corinthians 11:14, as "an angel of light."

Satan's desire was to drive a wedge between God and this perfect man He had made. Because Satan is God's enemy, he wanted to destroy God's relationship with this man who knew no suffering or sorrow and who had everything he needed. Satan could not bear to see this man have perfect fellowship with God. Satan himself once had fellowship with God for he had been created as Lucifer, but later he fell into sin by setting his will against God's will (Isa. 14:12-14).

Satan hates God and through the ages he has attempted to turn man away from God. God made man loving, so Satan appeared in the Garden to make him hateful. God made man humble, so Satan's goal was to make him proud. God wanted man to know only good, so Satan made it his purpose to see that man tasted evil.

Satan's desire was to convince Eve that she lacked something because she knew only good. This kind of thinking is still with us today. An example of this is those who say they do not want to send their children to a Christian elementary school because they do not want to make house plants out of them. I believe such reasoning is completely out of line for the Christian because that kind of logic originated in Genesis 3 with Satan. Satan said to man in the Garden of Eden, "God has made you a house plant. All you know is good. But you come with me and I will show you how you can be like God and know good and evil."

When presented to man in this way, evil's appeal was stronger than that of good. Man fell into sin and disobeyed God.

God made man to be obedient, so Satan said, "I will get him to disobey. I will cut man off and loose him from God so I can have him for myself." Satan wants man for himself; he wants man to serve him instead of God.

This was Satan's plot as he entered the Garden of Eden and beguiled and deceived the woman by suggesting that she act independently of God. In other words, he aroused her self-interest. She listened and yielded, and when she acted in self-interest she sinned. That sin separated her from God, but that was not all. Her sin also separated her from her husband. Since Adam had not yet eaten, Eve's fellowship was broken with him as well as with God. This left Adam alone in his fellowship with God. How long Adam and Eve remained in this broken fellowship we do not know because there is no time element mentioned in Genesis 3.

Adam's Deliberate Choice

Adam was in the middle. He desired to fellowship with God on the one hand, and he desired to fellowship with his wife on the other hand. Adam was alone in his fellowship with God, but his heart was drawn to his wife who had broken her fellowship with him and God. In order to have fellowship with one, Adam had to break fellowship with the other. His desire to have fellowship with the woman became greater than his desire to have fellowship with God, so he also ate

19

of the fruit and broke his fellowship with God. However, Adam was not deceived. Writing by inspiration in the New Testament, the Apostle Paul said, "Adam was not deceived, but the woman being deceived was in the transgression" (I Tim. 2:14). Adam's sin was the result of a deliberate choice. This is why the responsibility for sin was placed fully on him. His sin severed the life cord between God and man. Man had now chosen to be on Satan's side against God. Man himself became the enemy of God. Through this act of deliberate disobedience, man went from a God-centered life to a self-centered life; from a life which seeks to please God, to a life which seeks to please self.

God Makes Provision

Adam and Eve became estranged from God. Fellowship was broken. Now what would God do regarding man whom He created? In Genesis 3 we read of God seeking Adam and Eve after they had sinned. God still loved man. Even though man rebelled against God, this did not change God's love for him. Ephesians 2:4,5 tells us, "But God, who is rich in mercy, for his great love wherewith he loved us, Even when we were dead in sins, hath quickened us together with Christ, (by grace ye are saved;)." From these verses we see that God's love for man was never diminished even though man rejected Him. God loved Adam and Eve when they were dead in sin and He loved us when we were dead in sin.

Because of God's great love, He made a provision for man's sin. John 3:16 records the wonderful truth that "God so loved the world, that he gave his only begotten Son, that whosoever believeth in him should not perish, but have everlasting life." God never stopped loving man.

When God was seeking Adam and Eve in the Garden, they hid among the trees in an effort to escape from Him. Before their fellowship was broken by sin, they expectantly waited for God to visit them—but now they hid themselves. Satan was able to drive a wedge of sin between Adam and Eve and God which resulted in a breach of fellowship.

When God was seeking Adam, He called out, "Where art thou?" (v. 9). Adam answered, "I heard thy voice in the garden, and I was afraid, because I was naked; and I hid myself" (v. 10). This shows man's fallen condition, but God continued to seek him.

God determined to repair the damage that had been done. First, He placed a curse on Satan, the instigator of the sin. Because Satan had appeared in the form of a serpent, God said, "Because thou hast done this, thou art cursed above all cattle, and above every beast of the field; upon thy belly shalt thou go, and dust shalt thou eat all the days of thy life: And I will put enmity between thee and the woman, and between thy seed and her seed; it shall bruise thy head, and thou shalt bruise his heel."

God foretold that the seed of the woman would eventually completely crush and bruise Satan's head. The woman's "seed" refers to the Lord Jesus Christ. This was a prophecy that Christ would suffer yet He would be victorious over Satan.

On the cross, Christ suffered more than any man was able to suffer. The description of His suffering was prophesied in Isaiah 52:14: "Many were astonied at thee; his visage was so marred more than any man, and his form more than the sons of men." Christ was "despised and rejected of men; a man of sorrows, and acquainted with grief: and we hid as it were our faces from him; he was despised, and we esteemed him not" (Isa. 53:3). Why? Because "all we like sheep have gone astray; we have turned every one to his own way; and the Lord hath laid on him the iniquity of us all" (53:6). This is the suffering that God took upon Himself in behalf of man who had willfully rejected God's love and had been separated from Him. Of course, God's suffering for man includes you and me. Mankind suffers because of sin, but none of this compares to the suffering of the Lord Jesus Christ when He died to pay the penalty for our sin.

Because of Adam and Eve's sin, God drove them out of the Garden to a life of suffering and toil. But it was a life that brought greater suffering to God than to them. Oh, that we might realize the supreme suffering of God in our behalf. When we know this, we will realize that our suffering is but a trifle.

Man was caused to suffer that he might once more desire fellowship with God and enjoy His blessing. God provided for man's sin through the death of His Son on the cross. Christ suffered to atone—He suffered to pay the penalty for man's sin. Only through the suffering and death of Christ could man be reconciled to God. This truth is emphasized to us in II Corinthians 5:18 where we are told that God "hath reconciled us to himself by Jesus Christ."

22

But how long must the suffering last? It is wonderful to know that there is a termination to the suffering for both man and Christ. However, suffering will continue until Satan is banished, man's fellowship is restored, and all tears are wiped away. In Revelation 21:4 we are assured that "God shall wipe away all tears from their eyes; and there shall be no more death, neither sorrow, nor crying, neither shall there be any more pain: for the former things are passed away." In the following verse God tells us, "Behold, I make all things new." What a wonderful promise of God! This is what He has in store for us because of the supreme suffering of the Lord Jesus Christ.

Thought: Examine many of your troubles and you will find your own name stamped on them as the manufacturer.

Chapter 3

Christ, the Supreme Sufferer

Having traced suffering back to its source, we should never again be tempted to blame God for it. Especially is this true when we realize all the suffering that God has endured to deliver man from his suffering. Jesus Christ was without sin, yet He willingly accepted suffering and death to pay the penalty for our sin. Long before man was ever created, God knew what would happen. Therefore, He prepared a remedy for man's sin. Satan would not be able to spoil God's purpose for man very long. The plan for a complete remedy involved the highest cost to God. It was the suffering and death of His only begotten Son.

It is evident from I Peter 1:20 that God planned for man's redemption even before man was created. In referring to our redemption through the precious blood of Christ, this verse describes Christ as the One "who verily was foreordained before the foundation of the world, but was manifest in these last times for you."

Every person is in need of God's provision for sin because Adam's sin has been passed on to everyone. Romans 5:12 makes the solemn statement: "Wherefore, as by one man sin entered into the world, and death by sin; and so death passed upon all men, for that all have sinned." Romans 3:23 also confirms the fact that "all have sinned, and come short of the glory of God."

In the first Adam there is only death and suffering, but the last Adam—the Lord Jesus Christ—came to abolish death and suffering. In II Timothy 1:10 the Lord Jesus Christ is described as the One "who hath abolished death, and hath brought life and immortality to light through the gospel." Christ's suffering, as prophesied in Isaiah 53, was destined to end all suffering. It is because of what He accomplished by His death on the cross that God will be able to wipe away all tears, as recorded in Revelation 21:4.

Few people realize that it is the rejection of Christ's suffering in our behalf that is the cause of the world's mounting woes and suffering today. This suffering will increase because man continues to reject Jesus Christ as Saviour. There will be no decrease in the suffering until God has finally vindicated His Son, Jesus Christ.

This throws light on the mystery of suffering today. Suffering will continue and increase until it reaches its greatest intensity during the Great Tribulation. During these seven years, the suffering on earth will reach its greatest intensity. Those who continue to reject Jesus Christ as their Saviour will be cast into hell and will be eternally separated from God. Their suffering will continue forever and ever. Why? Because they rejected Jesus Christ who suffered in their behalf.

People constantly complain about the suffering and woes on earth today. Many ask the question, Doesn't God care? Yes, He cares. He cared enough to send His only begotten Son to suffer and die so that there might be an end to all suffering. Suffering is not the fault of God. It is the fault of man who chose to willfully go his own way against God's will. Sin is the cause of suffering. But even though Christ has suffered to pay the penalty for man's sin, men today continue to reject Him as Saviour. What Jesus said to the unbelievers in His day, He also says to the multitude of unbelievers today: "And ye will not come to me, that ye might have life" (John 5:40).

Christ's suffering was not because of His sin; it was for our sin. The greatest suffering that has ever been known to man was experienced by the Lord Jesus Christ. He suffered physically, mentally and spiritually that He might pay the penalty for sin—not His, but ours. He was forsaken of God for our sake. And His suffering will not be in vain. Those who receive Him as Saviour will have eternal life, and God will be vindicated against those who reject the suffering of His Son for their sin. Oh, that men might receive Jesus Christ as their Saviour and escape eternal condemnation.

Thought: Fellowship in Christ's suffering is the qualification for sharing in His dignity.

Chapter 4

The Christian's Assurance

When a Christian begins to suffer he frequently asks such questions as, Am I really saved? Is God allowing this? If I were really saved, would God let this kind of thing happen to me? One of the most important things to remember during times of suffering is that one of the reasons we suffer is because we are saved. The purpose of suffering in the Christian's life is to produce spiritual growth.

Assurance of Salvation

It is very important for every Christian to be sure of his salvation. Unless we understand the teaching about the assurance of salvation, we will not understand Christian suffering.

The Christian's standing before God is assured on the basis of the finished work of Christ. His death, burial and resurrection assure us of our salvation and right standing in the presence of God. This is emphasized by such verses as Ephesians 1:3 where the Apostle Paul exclaimed, "Blessed be the God and Father of our Lord Jesus Christ, who hath blessed us with all spiritual blessings in heavenly places in Christ." A similar verse is I Peter 1:3

which says, "Blessed be the God and Father of our Lord Jesus Christ, which according to his abundant mercy hath begotten us again unto a lively hope by the resurrection of Jesus Christ from the dead."

Both of these verses have the same opening phrase: "Blessed be the God and Father of our Lord Jesus Christ." And both of these verses deal with the Christian's standing before God. Notice the tense used here—God "hath blessed us" (Eph. 1:3) and He "hath begotten us again" (I Pet. 1:3).

In Ephesians 2:6 the Apostle Paul tells us that God "hath raised us up together, and made us sit together in heavenly places in Christ Jesus." Paul is not talking about a physical resurrection here because that would be in the future as far as his readers were concerned. But he makes it clear that the resurrection he is talking about has taken place in the past. We must remember that what God wills and begins is an already finished work to Him. *We* may begin something and be unable to finish it, but not so with God. As far as God is concerned, all the things He has purposed to do could be spoken of in the past tense to emphasize their certainty.

We refer to three time periods—past, present and future. But with God there is no such thing. He sees it all at one time. Although it is difficult for us to comprehend, we can praise the Lord that we serve such a God who is omnipotent and that when He wills something, it can already be spoken of as a past event.

Read the first chapter of Ephesians and notice that all the tenses—past, present and future—with God are already a finished thing. Note especially verses 4-7: "According as he hath chosen us in him

28

before the foundation of the world, that we should be holy and without blame before him in love: Having predestinated us unto the adoption of children by Jesus Christ to himself, according to the good pleasure of his will, To the praise of the glory of his grace, wherein he hath made us accepted in the beloved. In whom we have redemption through his blood, the forgiveness of sins, according to the riches of his grace."

If we have received Jesus Christ as Saviour, we are already accepted—that is a settled matter. With God it is a finished work. How wonderful this truth is for the Christian!

First Peter 1:3,4 tells us of our present position: "Blessed be the God and Father of our Lord Jesus Christ, which according to his abundant mercy hath begotten us again unto a lively hope by the resurrection of Jesus Christ from the dead, To an inheritance incorruptible, and undefiled, and that fadeth not away, reserved in heaven for you."

God has begotten us and He is going to finish that which He has begun. This refers to the new birth which, of course, is a spiritual birth. Christ spoke of this new birth when He said to Nicodemus, "Except a man be born again, he cannot see the kingdom of God" (John 3:3). John 1:12 emphasizes that we become children of God by receiving Christ as Saviour: "But as many as received him, to them gave he power to become the sons of God, even to them that believe on his name." All of salvation is God's doing. Second Corinthians 5:18 bears this out when it says, "All things are of God, who hath reconciled us to himself by Jesus Christ." All we need to do is to receive Christ as our Saviour.

God's Work Needs No Tests

Because salvation is a work of God, we may be sure that His work needs no trials or testings to see if it will endure or to see if it is any good. Too many times we relegate the power of God to the level of man's thinking. We use the trial and error method to see if something will work, and if it works we go ahead with it. God is not that way. He sees a work from its beginning to its end, so His is a finished work as far as He is concerned.

If we say that God is testing whether His creation is any good, we are taking away from His glory and power—we are making God like man. But God's work in our behalf is seen in the Scriptures as a finished work. He has blessed us in heavenly places in Christ and has seated us together with Christ. He also has an inheritance reserved for us in heaven and He will see us through to that inheritance.

In I Peter 1, we who are kept by the power of God are told of our inheritance reserved in heaven. We are also told: "Wherein ye greatly rejoice, though now for a season, if need be, ye are in heaviness through manifold temptations: That the trial of your faith, being much more precious than of gold that perisheth, though it be tried with fire, might be found unto praise and honour and glory at the appearing of Jesus Christ" (vv. 6,7). This emphasizes the Christian's earthly walk—that he is a pilgrim marching to glory and this sometimes takes him through suffering, tests and trials. But whatever the trial, each Christian is assured that the trial of his faith is much more precious than gold which perishes.

The important thing to see in all of this is that all is safe in heaven. Our inheritance is reserved for us. We must remember, then, that the testings and trials through which we are now passing can never change the fact that God has blessed us in heavenly places in Christ and that He has reserved an inheritance for us. Our standing is in Christ and it is secure because it all depends on Christ. Our standing remains unaltered, while our state or walk on earth is being matured. Our standing in Christ never changes, but our state does change as we develop in the Christian life while here on earth.

Colossians 3:2 exhorts each Christian, "Set your affection on things above, not on things on the earth. For ye are dead, and your life is hid with Christ in God." The words "for ye are dead" are literally, "for you died"—emphasizing a past act. The words "your life is hid with Christ in God" is literally, "your life has already been hidden with Christ in God." When a believer receives Christ as Saviour, his life becomes hidden with Christ in God. This remains true throughout the believer's life.

Whereas there has been death on the one hand, there has been life on the other hand. We died, but we have also been raised to our position with Christ. No one—no matter who they may be—can get at our position in Christ. They may kill us physically, but they cannot get at our spiritual life. In order to take away our spiritual life it would be necessary for them to destroy Christ and end His existence. He is our life. Since it will never be possible to destroy Him, it will never be possible to destroy our spiritual life.

Then the readers of Colossians are told, "When Christ, who is our life, shall appear, then shall ye also appear with him in glory" (3:4). This is the assurance that every believer has in Christ. The Book of Colossians goes on to tell how we should live on the earth by mortifying our members. This, however, refers to our state which is developing in maturity for Christ, but our standing in Christ is unchanging.

Progress of Assurance

Notice the progress of assurance as it is recorded in I Peter. It is beautiful to see how it is revealed in the Word of God. We see that God has begotten us again unto a lively hope (1:3). Later in the same chapter we are told, "Being born again, not of corruptible seed, but of incorruptible, by the word of God, which liveth and abideth for ever" (v. 23). Because God's Word lives and abides forever, and because of the new birth we have experienced, we will also live and abide forever.

The progress of the Christian life is also emphasized in Ephesians 2. Verses 8 and 9 tell us, "For by grace are ye saved through faith; and that not of yourselves: it is the gift of God: Not of works, lest any man should boast." However, we should not stop with verses 8 and 9 because God's purpose for us is revealed in verse 10: "For we are his workmanship, created in Christ Jesus unto good works, which God hath before ordained that we should walk in them." Verse 10 describes the results that are to follow salvation—good works. Verses 8 and 9 tell us the process of salvation, but verse 10 tells us the purpose of salvation.

The Believer's Assured Future

Believers are assured of many things, but three directly relate to the subject of why Christians suffer. First, every believer is assured that he has been begotten unto a "lively hope" (I Pet. 1:3). What is this lively hope? Part of the lively hope is our future bodily resurrection which is assured by the resurrection of Christ. Because Jesus was raised from the dead, every believer is assured that eventually he too will be physically raised from the dead. Why? Because our life is in Christ Jesus. Today we already have this resurrection life.

Titus 2:13 also tells us of our hope when it says, "Looking for that blessed hope, and the glorious appearing of the great God and our Saviour Jesus Christ." In the light of this wonderful truth, there is no room for despondency or being downcast. We are also encouraged when we read I John 3:2,3: "Beloved, now are we the sons of God, and it doth not yet appear what we shall be: but we know that, when he shall appear, we shall be like him; for we shall see him as he is. And every man that hath this hope in him purifieth himself, even as he is pure." All believers are assured in these verses that "now are we the sons of God." There is also the admonition for the believer: "And every man that hath this hope in him purifieth himself."

Second, the believer is also assured that he is born again "to an inheritance" (I Pet. 1:4). Not only is he born again unto a lively hope, but he is also born again unto an inheritance. There are four characteristics of this inheritance. It is "incorruptible." Death and corruption cannot

33

touch this inheritance which God has reserved for every believer. This inheritance is also "undefiled." It is not possible for anything to stain or defile it because it is in Christ Jesus. Also, the inheritance "fadeth not away." There is no inflationary devaluation here. This inheritance stays at full value—it doesn't fade away. In this life we see growth and development, and then a withering and passing away. But this inheritance in Christ never fades away. The fourth characteristic of this inheritance is that it is "reserved in heaven" for every Christian. This means that God is guarding it so it cannot be taken away.

This inheritance is in heaven now, awaiting our entering there. God guarantees the full value and He is guarding it just for us. We should not be discouraged no matter what physical suffering we experience on this earth, because there is coming a day when we shall have new bodies which will never experience suffering.

Kept by the Power of God

After describing the inheritance as being incorruptible, undefiled, not fading away and reserved in heaven for the Christians, the Apostle Peter describes Christians as those "who are kept by the power of God through faith unto salvation ready to be revealed in the last time" (I Pet. 1:5). Not only is our inheritance guarded by God, but we are also kept by His power. God keeps the inheritance for the believer, and He keeps the believer for the inheritance.

God has given every believer a proof that he will be kept unto that day when he will receive his inheritance. That proof is the Holy Spirit. God calls the proof the "earnest of our inheritance." This is emphasized for us in Ephesians 1:13,14: "In whom [Christ] ye also trusted, after that ye heard the word of truth, the gospel of your salvation: in whom also after that ye believed, ye were sealed with that holy Spirit of promise, Which is the earnest of our inheritance until the redemption of the purchased possession, unto the praise of his glory." The word "earnest" has such meanings as "first installment, deposit, down payment, pledge." Earnest money is still given today when it is necessary for the buyer to show that he is in earnest about making the final purchase.

The Holy Spirit has been given to the believer as God's guarantee that the rest of what He has for us will follow. God assures us that we will be kept for our inheritance. Whereas man may fail to make the necessary payments, God cannot fail for He is God.

First Peter 1:5 shows us the method God uses to keep us. We are kept "by the power of God through faith." All that God has for us is assured us the moment we, by faith, receive Jesus Christ as Saviour. It is then that we receive the Holy Spirit as the earnest of our inheritance. The moment we believe God, our faith is accepted by Him and that makes our inheritance sure. God first gives us faith (Eph. 2:8), then He keeps us by the faith He has given us.

Notice that the "salvation" of I Peter 1:5 is "ready to be revealed in the last time." Perhaps you say, What kind of salvation is this? I thought we had salvation now. The problem is solved when we see there are three aspects of salvation. These three aspects have to do with the past, present and future. First, there is deliverance from sin's penalty which took place when we received Christ as Saviour. Because we placed our faith in Him, we will never come into condemnation. Second, we are presently being delivered from the power and dominion of sin in our lives. This is the present process of our salvation. Third, we will be delivered from the presence of sin in the future. Just before the Lord Jesus Christ ascended to heaven, He told His disciples, "In my Father's house are many mansions: if it were not so, I would have told you. I go to prepare a place for you. And if I go and prepare a place for you, I will come again, and receive you unto myself; that where I am, there ye may be also" (John 14:2,3).

It is the third aspect of salvation—our future deliverance from the presence of sin—that I Peter 1:5 refers to. This third aspect of salvation is also emphasized in I Thessalonians 4:16,17: "For the Lord himself shall descend from heaven with a shout, with the voice of the archangel, and with the trump of God: and the dead in Christ shall rise first: Then we which are alive and remain shall be caught up together with them in the clouds, to meet the Lord in the air: and so shall we ever be with the Lord."

Another way to state the three aspects of salvation is that the salvation of the soul is in the past for the one who has received Christ as Saviour, the salvation of the life is taking place at the present, and the salvation of the body will take place in the future. Once a person receives Jesus Christ as his Saviour, the rest is guaranteed to him by God. God's guarantee is certain because He has guaranteed all of this to us "by the resurrection of Jesus Christ from the dead" (I Pet. 1:3). Because of Christ's resurrection we shall be resurrected also.

God has not only promised us an inheritance, He has also promised Jesus Christ an inheritance. This inheritance is mentioned in Ephesians 1:18 where the Apostle Paul prayed, "That ye may know what is the hope of his calling, and what the riches of the glory of his inheritance in the saints." Jesus Christ's inheritance will be the saints themselves! The believers during the Church Age are the true Church which is the Bride of Christ. We are God's gift to Christ for what He has done. So we are guarded and kept lest the Lord Jesus Christ should miss His inheritance.

Thought: God is satisfied with the cross as settling the sin question; we should be satisfied with what satisfies God.

Chapter 5

Joy in the Midst of Testing

Having assured the Christians that they would be kept for their inheritance, the Apostle Peter added, "Wherein ye greatly rejoice, though now for a season, if need be, ye are in heaviness through manifold temptations" (I Pet. 1:6). Here we have a great paradox. "Greatly rejoice . . . ye are in heaviness through manifold temptations." How can we greatly rejoice when we are in heaviness through many temptations? In what are we to rejoice?

We are to rejoice in the salvation mentioned in verse 5—the future aspect of our salvation which will be completed when we are delivered from the presence of sin. The Apostle Paul wrote that the entire creation is groaning and travailing in pain, waiting for this final redemption (Rom. 8:22,23).

From the Book of the Revelation we see that the believer will have a future enthronement with Christ after he has experienced the redemption of the body. Christ Himself said, "To him that overcometh will I grant to sit with me in my throne, even as I also overcame, and am set down with my Father in his throne" (3:21). We are overcomers because we have placed our faith in

Jesus Christ as our Saviour. First John 5:4,5 emphasizes this: "For whatsoever is born of God overcometh the world: and this is the victory that overcometh the world, even our faith. Who is he that overcometh the world, but he that believeth that Jesus is the Son of God?" However, there is another aspect of overcoming. It is in the believer's daily life and for this he is given rewards at the Judgment Seat of Christ. To sit with Christ in His throne will be the reward for those who overcome in Him.

In I Peter 4:12,13 we are told, "Beloved, think it not strange concerning the fiery trial which is to try you, as though some strange thing happened unto you: But rejoice, inasmuch as ye are partakers of Christ's sufferings; that, when his glory shall be revealed, ye may be glad also with exceeding joy." The purpose of our being partakers of Christ's sufferings is so that when His glory is revealed we can be glad with exceeding joy.

Although it is a paradox, the Christian is to rejoice even when he experiences suffering. Only the Christian can experience this. The paradox is better understood when we understand the difference between joy and sorrow.

Joy is something that is inward and is based on a solid foundation. For the believer this foundation is the Bible which tells us of Christ's finished work with its eternal results. Joy is based on something that God has done within us.

Whereas joy is inward, sorrow is outward. It is based on circumstances. These are transitory; they are temporary; they are for a season. So God tells the Christian that it is possible for him to rejoice even though he is passing through many or various kinds of testings. Thus the Christian is able to rejoice even in the midst of sorrow.

There is also a difference between joy and happiness. Happiness is based on happenings. It depends on circumstances. But even though the Christian is unhappy over circumstances, he can have the joy of the Lord in spite of the circumstances. Most people do not experience joy in the midst of adverse circumstances but God has made it possible for them to do so. Sorrow is also caused by happenings but it need never affect our joy, because joy does not depend on circumstances. It depends on what Christ has done. Joy is conditioned on our soul's relationship to the Lord and it is applied by faith.

Duration of Tests

As we consider I Peter 1:6 we see that there is a limitation to the tests because they are "for a season." They are not forever but are of limited duration. We also notice that there are "manifold temptations." The word translated "manifold" means "of various kinds, diversified." The word "temptation" means "testing." So for the Christian there will be various kinds of testing in his life.

Regardless of the kind of testing, we must always remember the promise of I Corinthians 10:13. This is also a verse which you should memorize so it can be recalled at any time. In this verse each Christian is promised, "There hath no temptation taken you but such as is common to man: but God is faithful, who will not suffer [permit] you to be tempted above that ye are able;

but will with the temptation also make a way to escape, that ye may be able to bear it."

Temptations or trials are the common lot of man, but God is always faithful. We need to learn to depend on His faithfulness. It is not merely our faith that is important, but our faith in His faithfulness. It is the object of our faith that makes the difference.

So God tells us in His Word that the testing in our lives will be temporary because it will come when it is needed and where it is needed. This is also emphasized by the words "if need be" in I Peter 1:6: "Wherein ye greatly rejoice, though now for a season, if need be, ye are in heaviness through manifold temptations." Some will be tested more than others for everyone will not have the same need.

When we read Hebrews 11:35-38 we see what some of the heroes of the faith suffered: "Others were tortured, not accepting deliverance; that they might obtain a better resurrection: And others had trial of cruel mockings and scourgings, yea, moreover of bonds and imprisonment: They were stoned, they were sawn asunder, were tempted, were slain with the sword: they wandered about in sheepskins and goatskins; being destitute, afflicted, tormented; (Of whom the world was not worthy:) they wandered in deserts, and in mountains, and in dens and caves of the earth." Some of God's people have greatly suffered for their faith. But for those who suffer there are the reassuring words of James 1:2 where the apostle wrote: "My brethren, count it all joy when ye fall into divers [various kinds of] temptations." We are to have joy because

41

of what the various kinds of testings will accomplish in our lives.

Because there are various kinds of testings, no two may be alike. Not only does testing come when we need it, but we are also given the very kind of testing we need. God calls some Christians to greater responsibility so He gives them greater testing. Others, because they may be walking far from the Lord, may have great testing also. But regardless of the kind of testing, we can always rejoice because of what it will accomplish in us and because it is only for a season.

Thought: Keep your face always toward the sunshine, and the shadows will fall behind you.

Chapter 6

The Trial of Faith

The Apostle Peter made it clear in his first epistle that the reason for the "manifold temptations" was "that the trial of your faith, being much more precious than of gold that perisheth, though it be tried with fire, might be found unto praise and honour and glory at the appearing of Jesus Christ" (1:7). Notice especially the phrase "the trial of your faith." Faith is the foundation for all spiritual living. If faith stands, everything else will stand. If faith fails, all else will fail. Everything in the spiritual realm depends on faith.

Faith is much more important even in the physical realm than we usually consider it to be. The farmer plants his crop and by faith he expects the seed to produce. Certainly he has seen it happen before but he still has to trust and have confidence that it will happen again, or else he would never plant the crop. Trust is needed in all areas of life. We trust the economy of our country and evidence this trust by investing our money in various places. Faith—there must be faith in everything. Because faith is so crucial, it must be

43

put to the test to prove whether it is genuine or imitation.

There is a great difference between faith and feeling. It is evident by the way we live that many of us have not learned the difference. Faith is totally based on the Word of God. Romans 10:17 tells us that "faith cometh by hearing, and hearing by the word of God." The Word of God is the only place where we can get faith as far as the Person and work of God is concerned.

On the other hand, feelings are based on circumstances. I remember having prayed a long time about a certain amount of money which we needed for one of the Back to the Bible ministries. As I prayed, there came a time when I did not feel that the amount of money would be coming. This feeling came about because I had been praying for some time and the money had not come. Finally, I had to settle the matter of feelings with the Lord and say, "Lord, I do not feel like the money is going to come, but I know that feeling has nothing to do with faith." Then I went to the Word of God and, based on His promises, I said, "I will believe this in spite of how I feel." Thank the Lord, He responded to faith and sent the amount of money that was needed to do His work. Faith is based on the Word of God, but feelings depend on circumstances.

Peter emphasized that the trial of our faith is "much more precious than of gold that perisheth" (1:7). Our faith is precious because faith procures all from God. On the basis of faith we get what we need for this life. Faith is more precious than gold or the things of this life because they perish, but faith does not. Faith not only procures what we

44

need for this life, but it procures heaven with its rewards and blessings. When all the things of this life are passed away, faith will bring to fruition that which is real and of far greater value.

Our faith is much more precious than gold even though the gold has been purified or "tried with fire" (I Pet. 1:7). Just as gold has to be purified by fire to bring out that which is good, so also our faith has to be tested to be purified and approved by God.

Job's faith was tested just as severely as gold is tested. In the midst of his suffering, Job said, "But he [God] knoweth the way that I take: when he hath tried me, I shall come forth as gold" (23:10). Job had confidence in God even in the midst of severe physical suffering and mental anguish. His mental anguish resulted from the opposition and false accusations of his friends. Although Job wavered for a moment, he later turned to God with even more certainty.

Job did not have all the answers and God seemed far off. This is evident from Job's words: "Behold, I go forward, but he is not there; and backward, but I cannot perceive him: On the left hand, where he doth work, but I cannot behold him: he hideth himself on the right hand, that I cannot see him" (23:8,9). Job did not know why God had permitted such suffering to come to him, but he was certain that after he had been tried he would come forth as gold. That is faith. Job received comfort when he realized anew that God was working with him and that even though he did not understand his circumstances, God knew everything. Job had confidence that God knew the

45

way he was taking and that He had not forsaken him.

Perhaps in your sufferings and trials you too have found that sometimes God seems far from you. At such times it will seem very dark and discouraging. But always remember, God knows where you are and He knows how much you are suffering. God knows what He is doing with you and where He is leading you. As Job, you can be confident that after God has tried you, you will come forth as gold. So look beyond your trials; look to God. You may not feel that all is right but you cannot depend on your feelings. You may not be happy either, but remember that happiness, like feelings, depends on circumstances. Look to God in faith, and this will bring you the answer. According to Hebrews 11:1, "Faith is the substance of things hoped for, the evidence of things not seen." Faith is already having what we believe. Such faith enables us to base our present lives on that which we will receive in the future.

God's Perfect Knowledge

God has perfect knowledge of your life and my life. As Job said, "He knoweth the way that I take" (23:10). Later, Job said of God, "For his eyes are upon the ways of man, and he seeth all his goings. There is no darkness, nor shadow of death, where the workers of iniquity may hide themselves. For he will not lay upon man more than right; that he should enter into judgment with God" (34:21-23). Notice what Job realized! God does not bring more on a person than is right. If God did this, man **could** enter into judgment with

46

God and say, "God is mistreating me." The Lord knows the suffering that every person is experiencing. The Book of Proverbs tells us that "the eyes of the Lord are in every place, beholding the evil and the good" (15:3). There is not a single thing in our lives that escapes God's attention.

When you realize that God knows all about you, does this thought disturb or comfort you? Those who are living in sin shrink back when they think of God's knowledge. If fear strikes your heart when you think of the fact that God knows everything about you, this indicates that you are not right with the Lord. When there is sin in the life it is a terrible thought to know that God has full knowledge of every detail of your life. If your heart is not right with the Lord you need to confess your sin to Him. We are assured in I John 1:9 that "if we confess our sins, he [God] is faithful and just to forgive us our sins, and to cleanse us from all unrighteousness."

If you are comforted by the thought that God knows all about you, it is an indication that you are walking uprightly and in fellowship with the Lord. You are pleased to realize that God knows all about your trials, difficulties, sorrows, efforts—and even failures. God knows and understands even though your friends may not. Job's friends thought he was a hypocrite and your friends may feel you are a great sinner because of some of the trials you are suffering. They may think your suffering is the result of some hidden sin and they may talk behind your back. Job's friends were open with their false accusations, but this is often not true of friends of the suffering Christian. People seem anxious to attribute God's

47

trials to evil they think may be in us. But be assured that God knows the truth. Proverbs 20:24 says, "Man's goings are of the Lord; how can a man then understand his own way?" Or as Jeremiah said, "O Lord, I know that the way of man is not in himself: it is not in man that walketh to direct his steps. O Lord, correct me, but with judgment; not in thine anger, lest thou bring me to nothing" (Jer. 10:23,24). In other words, Jeremiah was saying, "If You need to judge me, Lord, then do it—but do it in mercy and kindness."

God Has a Purpose

Job said, "When he hath tried me" (23:10). Job realized it was God who was doing the trying. How wonderful it was that Job understood this fact. In Jeremiah 17:10 the Lord tells us, "I the Lord search the heart, I try the reins, even to give every man according to his ways, and according to the fruit of his doings." God says, "I do all of this."

In the midst of our suffering, we must always remember that God has a purpose for what we are experiencing. This was evident even in the testing of Israel, for God said through Moses, "And thou shalt remember all the way which the Lord thy God led thee these forty years in the wilderness, to humble thee, and to prove thee, to know what was in thine heart, whether thou wouldest keep his commandments, or no" (Deut. 8:2). God's purpose for testing the Israelites was to prove them, to know what was in their hearts and whether they would keep His commandments. God always has a purpose in testing us. He is testing and proving our faith. He is humbling us before Him. When we realize this, we will bear up better under the trials we are experiencing. The realization that God has a purpose in our suffering will give us more patience to endure trials. The irritations of life will be less when we know that God is testing us for a purpose.

God tests our tempers, our courage, our faith, our patience, our love, our fidelity. He is testing us to see what our real attitudes are. Perhaps you have been experiencing serious trial in one of these areas. But no matter how severe your testing has been, be sure to remember I Corinthians 10:13. God is faithful to make a way of escape so we may be able to bear the testing.

Our need is to believe God—to trust Him. Too often we blame Satan for our tests and trials. Certainly, Satan brings about much harassment in our Christian lives, but we must always remember that Satan cannot touch us without God's approval. God is above all principalities and powers and they cannot move without His permission. Satan may be used of God as an instrument for testing, but only to the degree that God permits. And you may be assured that God will not permit you to be tested beyond what you are able to bear. Job recognized this. He knew he would not be tested beyond his breaking point.

Therefore, let us look beyond the instrument of testing—beyond the Devil—to God who "worketh all things after the counsel of his own will" (Eph. 1:11). God knows what He is doing. Job learned this and we need to learn it also.

Notice Job's response to his suffering: "Then Job arose, and rent his mantle, and shaved his head, and fell down upon the ground, and

49

worshipped" (1:20). When did he worship? After he had lost everything he had—family, servants, and all his possessions. Job responded to his losses by saying, "Naked came I out of my mother's womb, and naked shall I return thither; the Lord gave, and the Lord hath taken away; blessed be the name of the Lord" (v. 21). This was the text we claimed when God took our firstborn to heaven.

The divine commentary on Job's actions and attitude is found in verse 22: "In all this Job sinned not, nor charged God foolishly."

Even though Job was tried and afflicted almost more than any other man, he never lost confidence in God. Job said, "He knoweth the way that I take: when he hath tried me, I shall come forth as gold" (23:10).

Because faith is the foundation of all spiritual living—everything in the spiritual realm depends on it—faith must be put to the test. It must be proved, verified. You must be tested to prove whether you really have faith which will be able to procure for you everything you need spiritually.

In the midst of his sufferings, Job looked ahead and said, "I shall come forth as gold" (23:10). Job knew what would result from his testing. Though he lived centuries before I Peter 1:7 was written, he knew the truth stated in it: "That the trial of your faith, being much more precious than of gold that perisheth, though it be tried with fire, might be found unto praise and honour and glory at the appearing of Jesus Christ." They say that when gold is purified, the purifier is able to look into it and see his image reflected. This was what Job knew would happen in his life. It wasn't that Job hoped or thought he might come forth as gold, but to him it was a certainty: "I shall come forth as gold." Oh, that we might have such certainty about God and His purposes in our lives.

How could Job be so sure of the outcome of his testing? He could be sure because he knew God's purpose could not fail. We too are assured of this in such verses as Ephesians 1:3 which tells us that God "hath blessed us with all spiritual blessings in heavenly places in Christ." These blessings are so certain that they are referred to in the past tense. While many of these blessings are yet future for us, as far as God is concerned they are finished transactions.

In Philippians 1:6 we are assured, "Being confident of this very thing, that he which hath begun a good work in you will perform it until the day of Jesus Christ." This verse is often misquoted by well-meaning friends who write us and say, "God has begun a good work through you—the Back to the Bible Broadcast—and He will finish it." However, Philippians 1:6 is not talking about a good work God does "through" you, but a work He does "in" you. This is something God is doing to perfect you and to prepare you for all eternity. Thus He can say, "I have begun it and I will see it through."

The psalmist said, "The Lord will perfect that which concerneth me: thy mercy, O Lord, endureth for ever: forsake not the works of thine own hands" (138:8). What God begins He will see through to the end. This same truth is emphasized in Hebrews 13:20,21 which records the benediction: "Now the God of peace, that brought again from the dead our Lord Jesus, that great

51

shepherd of the sheep, through the blood of the everlasting covenant, Make you perfect in every good work to do his will, working in you that which is wellpleasing in his sight, through Jesus Christ; to whom be glory for ever and ever. Amen."

Paul's Confidence

The Apostle Paul was convinced that God was able to complete what He had begun. Paul emphasized this truth concerning his own life when he said, "Not as though I had already attained, either were already perfect: but I follow after, if that I may apprehend that for which also I am apprehended of Christ Jesus. Brethren, I count not myself to have apprehended: but this one thing I do, forgetting those things which are behind, and reaching forth unto those things which are before, I press toward the mark for the prize of the high calling of God in Christ Jesus (Phil. 3:12-14). Jesus Christ had apprehended Paul on the road to Damascus and Paul knew that what had begun in his life would continue to the end. Because Paul had his eyes set on what God was going to do for him, he forgot all that was behind—which included many trials and tests.

Because of Paul's confidence in God he was able to write in II Timothy 1:12, "I know whom I have believed, and am persuaded that he is able to keep that which I have committed unto him against that day." In other words, Paul was saying, "I know what God is able to do. I know He is able to keep. Because I know His purpose, I commit my whole being to Him." Oh, that we might have the same confidence in God.

Thought: God would have no furnaces if there were no gold to separate from the dross.

Chapter 7

Why God Permits Suffering

Although many think that sin is the only reason that Christians suffer, when we study the Word of God we see there are several reasons why God permits suffering.

Chastening

Chapter 12 of the Book of Hebrews gives us many significant truths about the matter of suffering. It is in this chapter that we are told, "For whom the Lord loveth he chasteneth, and scourgeth every son whom he receiveth. If ye endure chastening, God dealeth with you as with sons; for what son is he whom the father chasteneth not? But if ye be without chastisement, whereof all are partakers, then are ye bastards, and not sons. Furthermore we have had fathers of our flesh which corrected us, and we gave them reverence: shall we not much rather be in subjection unto the Father of spirits, and live? For they verily for a few days chastened us after their own pleasure; but he for our profit, that we might be partakers of his holiness" (vv. 6-10). God chastens us for our profit that we might be partakers of His holiness.

From Hebrews 12 we see that chastening is a heavenly discipline. The word "chasten" means "to train by correcting." The word "chasten" does not emphasize punishment as much as it emphasizes correction. This is especially true regarding the chastening of the Lord. The sufferings which the Lord permits are not punitive but corrective. Many people have asked, "What have I now done that God is punishing me?" Such questions disappear when we realize that for the Christian suffering is not for punishment but for correction.

It is clear from verses 7 and 8 of Hebrews 12 that chastening is an evidence that God has recognized us as sons. Earthly fathers chasten their sons to bring out the best in them. So also, God chastens us because He wants us to amount to something. God wants to bring out the potential that He sees in us. He has made us and He wants to mature us so we might become useful to Him.

But also notice that if there is no chastening then we have reason for discouragement. An absence of chastening means we are not sons—we are bastards. In other words, we are outside of the family of God. We may call ourselves "Christians" but we are not born again if we are not experiencing chastening. So when chastening comes we should be encouraged rather than discouraged because it indicates we are the sons of God.

Consider the contrast between divine punishment and divine chastisement. The Christian cannot be punished for sins because the punishment for his sins was poured out on the cross. Hebrews 10:10 says, "By the which will we are sanctified [set apart through salvation] through the offering of the body of Jesus Christ once for all."

We are assured in I John 1:7 that "if we walk in the light, as he is in the light, we have fellowship one with another, and the blood of Jesus Christ his Son cleanseth us from all sin." Verse 9 of this same chapter says, "If we confess our sins, he is faithful and just to forgive us our sins, and to cleanse us from all unrighteousness." This is where the chastisement comes in—cleansing from all unrighteousness. We confess and He forgives on the basis of His finished atonement, but He may send chastisement to cleanse us.

That the Christian is not punished is made clear in Romans 8:1: "There is therefore now no condemnation to them which are in Christ Jesus." Why? Because Christ has already suffered the condemnation. God will not punish a person the second time for the same sins. Jesus took all our sins on Him on the cross and when we receive Him as Saviour we are delivered from all further judgment. Jesus Christ Himself emphasized this when He said, "He that heareth my word, and believeth on him that sent me, hath everlasting life, and shall not come into condemnation; but is passed from death unto life" (John 5:24). This is not a license to sin. To think that this frees us to sin will only bring more chastisement upon us.

As a Judge God punishes, but as a Father He chastises. He is our Judge until we receive Christ as Saviour. We cannot call Him Father until we become His children. John 1:12 tells us that "as many as received him, to them gave he power to become the sons of God, even to them that believe on his name."

The idea that everyone is a child of God is simply not true. We are all God's by creation, but we are not all His children. We only become His children when we are born into His family. God judges those who are outside His family, but He chastises those who are in His family in order to bring out the best in them.

Divine punishment is never sent for the good of a sinner, but to honor God's law and to vindicate His government. Divine chastisement, however, is sent for the well-being of the children of God. It is sent for our profit that we might be partakers of His holiness. Notice the difference—punishment is necessary to vindicate God's law, but chastisement is for the good of His children. Punishment is never for man's good because it only separates him from God. But chastisement proceeds from God's love for those who are His children.

If we are experiencing God's chastisement, this is His proof that He loves us as sons. It can become a great blessing to us if we realize this truth. We are to receive chastisement with thanksgiving for God says, "In every thing give thanks: for this is the will of God in Christ Jesus concerning you" (I Thess. 5:18). Yes, we are even to give thanks for the sufferings. Because we are human it is hard to do this, but we need to look at it from God's viewpoint and say, "Thank You, Lord. I am so glad You have made it clear that I am Your child and that You are working in me to bring me to maturity."

Kinds of Chastening

Disciplinary chastening is illustrated by David's life. He committed grievous sins in the latter part of his life and was disciplined. Read his own words in Psalm 32:3,4: "When I kept silence, my bones waxed old through my roaring all the day long. For day and night thy hand was heavy upon me: my moisture is turned into the drought of summer." This was David's expression after his sin when God dealt with him and disciplined him. In Psalm 119:67 David said, "Before I was afflicted I went astray: but now have I kept thy word." In verse 71 of this same Psalm David said, "It is good for me that I have been afflicted; that I might learn thy statutes." So then, David's affliction was disciplinary.

However, we see that not all chastening is disciplinary when we recall the story of Job. He was a self-satisfied, self-righteous type of good Christian. His chastisement was *corrective* that he might be a greater partaker of God's holiness. Job himself recorded the results of his suffering when he wrote, "I have heard of thee by the hearing of the ear: but now mine eye seeth thee. Wherefore I abhor myself, and repent in dust and ashes" (Job 42:5,6).

Then consider Abraham. His trials were not because of any open sin or for correcting inward faults, but rather for developing spiritual graces. In Abraham's life the chastening was *educative*. He was tested in order to strengthen his faith and to produce patience. He was weaned from the things of the world so he might have closer fellowship with Jehovah. He thus became the "friend of

58

God." Why? Because he recognized what God was doing for him. James 2:23 tells us that "Abraham believed God, and it was imputed unto him for righteousness: and he was called the Friend of God."

Then there was the Apostle Paul whose chastening was not disciplinary, corrective or educative, but *preventive*. The purpose of Paul's suffering is found in his own words in II Corinthians 12:7: "And lest I should be exalted above measure through the abundance of the revelations, there was given to me a thorn in the flesh, the messenger of Satan to buffet me, lest I should be exalted above measure." Here was a man who had received so much revelation from God that there was a danger he would become proud. God knew what might happen so He gave Paul a "thorn in the flesh" to keep him from becoming proud. Paul was made and kept conscious of his own weakness. Three times Paul besought the Lord to remove his thorn in the flesh, but God said to him, "My grace is sufficient for thee: for my strength is made perfect in weakness" (v. 9). Paul's response to his suffering is found in the last part of verse 9: "Most gladly therefore will I rather glory in my infirmities, that the power of Christ may rest upon me."

How can we diagnose whether chastening in the lives of others is disciplinary, corrective, educative or preventive? It is impossible. Therefore, we must not pronounce judgment on why others are being chastened of the Lord. For my personal attitude in this matter I have found Paul's words to be very instructive: "As for me, myself, it is of very little concern to me to be examined by you or any human court; in fact, I do not even examine myself. For although my conscience does not accuse me, yet I am not entirely vindicated by that. It is the Lord Himself who must examine me. So you must stop forming any premature judgments, but wait until the Lord shall come again; for He will bring to light the secrets hidden in the dark and will make known the motives of men's hearts, and the proper praise will be awarded each of us" (I Cor. 4:3-5, *Wms.*).

Since there are many reasons for suffering, we cannot pronounce judgment on a person who is under the rod of God. Perhaps that person knows the reason, but we do not know. Some people seem to suffer much more than others—perhaps because God is preparing them for something very great, either on earth or in heaven.

Purifying

Another reason that God permits suffering is mentioned in Malachi 3:3: "And he shall sit as a refiner and purifier of silver: and he shall purify the sons of Levi, and purge them as gold and silver, that they may offer unto the Lord an offering in righteousness." God is a refiner.

The penalty for sin has been paid so there is no condemnation, but sin has corrupted our nature so it must be cleansed. Sin has polluted us so we must be purged. Sin has marred the divine image of God in us so it must be restored. This is what God is doing in our lives. Can we expect that all of this will be done without suffering?

According to Romans 8:28,29, God is using various processes to purify us. These verses tell us,

"We know that all things work together for good to them that love God, to them who are the called according to his purpose. For whom he did foreknow, he also did predestinate to be conformed to the image of his Son, that he might be the firstborn among many brethren." God is restoring the image. Receiving Christ as Saviour takes care of the condemnation of sin, but suffering by God's permission is necessary for a complete transformation of our living. Only then will we be well fitted and prepared—not only for this life but also for the life to come.

In Isaiah 48:10 God says, "I have chosen thee in the furnace of affliction." The furnace referred to is the kind used to refine gold and silver. Such a furnace was not for suffering, but for separation.

Because of the Fall in the Garden of Eden, man became a mixture of good and evil, so it became necessary for God to separate the dross and take it out. This is why God is viewed as a purifier in the Old Testament. God says in Isaiah 1:25, "I will turn my hand upon thee, and purely purge away thy dross, and take away all thy tin." Or as we have seen in Malachi 3:3, God sits as a purifier so that those who are purified may offer unto Him an offering in righteousness. How intense must the heat be in order for God to purify? How long must it last? These things depend on God and how long it takes Him to see His image in the gold being purified. God watches with carefulness and, according to I Corinthians 10:13, He will not test us beyond that which we are able to bear. God watches until He sees the total image of Christ in us. The real purpose of suffering has to do with eternity. Suffering is for a time. It is short. But through it, God prepares the Christian for eternity.

Have you ever watched a threshing machine separate the grain from the chaff? The grain and straw go through the machine and get pounded and almost hammered to pieces. Why? To separate the chaff from the grain. It is necessary for God to spiritually put us through the separator so the chaff in our lives may be separated from that which is really important.

In the Scriptures, God's work with His child is also likened to a potter's work with his clay. Jeremiah recorded the words of the Lord when he wrote, "The word which came to Jeremiah from the Lord, saying, Arise, and go down to the potter's house, and there I will cause thee to hear my words. Then I went down to the potter's house, and, behold, he wrought a work on the wheels. And the vessel that he made of clay was marred in the hand of the potter: so he made it again another vessel, as seemed good to the potter to make it. Then the word of the Lord came to me, saying, O house of Israel, cannot I do with you as this potter? saith the Lord. Behold, as the clay is in the potter's hand, so are ye in mine hand, O house of Israel" (Jer. 18:1-6). These words were spoken to Israel but they have an application to us. As a potter, God has us in His hand to mold us into that which He pleases. Perhaps you say that the treatment of the potter is too severe. Remember Job. It was said of him that he was a godly man, but God wanted to shape him into a vessel that would bring even more honor to Him.

I once heard about a bar of iron that, in the rough, was worth about a dollar. But after it had been heated, hammered and processed over and over again, it was made into needles worth about $70. The same bar of iron might have been made into watch springs worth thousands of dollars. But none of this would be possible without the extreme processes through which it passed. God wants to make us of more worth to Him and that is why the trial of our faith is much more precious than gold that perishes. Fire separates the dross.

We are also told about suffering in I Peter 4:1,2: "Forasmuch then as Christ hath suffered for us in the flesh, arm yourselves likewise with the same mind: for he that hath suffered in the flesh hath ceased from sin; That he no longer should live the rest of his time in the flesh to the lusts of men, but to the will of God." The phrase "hath ceased from sin" does not mean that the believer will never again commit an act of sin. It means that the believer has been released from the power of sin. This same truth is brought out in Romans 6:14: "For sin shall not have dominion over you: for ye are not under the law, but under grace."

Fruit Bearing

Another reason that God permits suffering in the lives of His children is that they might bring forth more fruit. Jesus Christ Himself said, "Every branch in me that beareth not fruit he taketh away: and every branch that beareth fruit, he purgeth it, that it may bring forth more fruit" (John 15:2). Notice the wonderful results of this purging—"more fruit" and then "much fruit." In verse 8 of this chapter the Lord Jesus Christ said, "Herein is my Father glorified, that ye bear much fruit; so shall ye be my disciples."

God permits suffering so we might bring forth much fruit. It is to be fruit unto righteousness such as we read in Hebrews 12:11: "Now no chastening for the present seemeth to be joyous, but grievous: nevertheless afterward it yieldeth the peaceable fruit of righteousness unto them which are exercised thereby." Notice that the "peaceable fruit of righteousness" is produced only by those who are "exercised thereby." How are we exercised thereby? By submitting. We are to submit thankfully and God will work out His righteousness in us so we will bear much fruit.

Perfecting

God also permits His children to suffer so He might perfect them; that is, that He might make them spiritually mature. First Peter 5:10 tells us about this: "But the God of all grace, who hath called us unto his eternal glory by Christ Jesus, after that ye have suffered a while, make you perfect, stablish, strengthen, settle you." Here we see four important results of suffering.

First, through suffering God is able to *perfect* us. The word which is translated "perfect" means "complete" or "make complete." Thus we can see that God wants to bring about a spiritual maturity in our lives.

Second, God wants to *stablish* us through suffering. Too many Christians are unstable. When the weather is good, they feel good; but when the weather is bad, they feel bad. They have no stability in their Christian lives. Thus, through suffering God wants to establish us—cause us to be more stable.

Third, God wants to *strengthen* us through suffering. Trials strengthen us in that when the next trial comes we are able to face it a little easier. Little by little, greater trials are sent and we find we are able to bear them. Remember Abraham? First, he was asked to leave his country and his home. Later, he had to separate himself from Lot—the only one of his family that was with him. Then he had to wait a long time for the birth of his son Isaac. This in itself was great suffering. Then when Isaac was born and had grown to be a young man, Abraham was called on to offer him as a sacrifice. Trial upon trial; one seeming to build on another. But in all of this, Abraham was strengthened in his faith and became an example to us who believe.

Fourth, through suffering God wants to *settle* us. This was the result of Abraham's tests—he became a mature man of God and became settled in his faith in God. Too many Christians are either up or down. On one day they have a mountaintop experience but on the next day they are down in the valley. One time they are on top of the circumstances but a short time later they are under the circumstances. Crops fail or sickness comes to the family and there is despair and a questioning of why God allows such.

God wants and needs even-keel Christians. Only those who are mature, established, strengthened and settled will be able to stand in the spiritual warfare. That the Christian is engaged in a spiritual warfare is made clear in Ephesians 6:12,13: "For we wrestle not against flesh and blood, but against principalities, against powers,

65

against the rulers of the darkness of this world, against spiritual wickedness in high places. Wherefore take unto you the whole armour of God, that ye may be able to withstand in the evil day, and having done all, to stand."

Disposing of Self

God also permits suffering in the lives of His children to dispose of self. Each Christian must learn that it is "not I, but Christ." Suffering reveals this to us—especially when we have failed along the way. Out of his suffering, the Apostle Paul was able to write, "I am crucified with Christ: nevertheless I live; yet not I, but Christ liveth in me: and the life which I now live in the flesh I live by the faith of the Son of God, who loved me, and gave himself for me" (Gal. 2:20). It was also the Apostle Paul who wrote, "For the love of Christ constraineth us; because we thus judge, that if one died for all, then were all dead: And that he died for all, that they which live should not henceforth live unto themselves, but unto him which died for them, and rose again" (II Cor. 5:14,15). Because of what Paul had suffered, self had been so disposed of that he was able to write, "For to me to live is Christ, and to die is gain" (Phil. 1:21).

Thus the mature, tested Christian life is the "unselfed life." Self seeks for its own rights, but suffering changes the center of one's life from "I" to "others." This is emphasized in II Corinthians 1:4 which says that the God of all comfort "comforteth us in all our tribulation, that we may be able to comfort them which are in any trouble, by the comfort wherewith we ourselves are comforted of God." Suffering teaches us to suffer with others.

Presenting Believers Faultless

God permits suffering in the lives of His children so they might be presented faultless in His presence. Jude alluded to this presentation when he said, "Now unto him that is able to keep you from falling, and to present you faultless before the presence of his glory with exceeding joy" (v. 24). The Apostle Paul also referred to this presentation of the Church to Christ when he wrote, "That he might sanctify and cleanse it with the washing of water by the word, That he might present it to himself a glorious church, not having spot, or wrinkle, or any such thing; but that it should be holy and without blemish" (Eph. 5:26,27).

Through suffering God is preparing us so we might be presented to Him faultless—without spot or wrinkle. Through God's work in our lives there will be no shortcomings when we are presented to Him.

Suffering Will Be Compensated

Having considered why God permits suffering in the lives of His children, we must never forget that God will compensate all suffering through which His children pass. Nothing will be forgotten. God keeps the books. The psalmist said, "Thou tellest my wanderings: put thou my tears into thy bottle: are they not in thy book?" (Ps. 56:8). In other words, the psalmist had confidence that God

67

was fully aware of his suffering and had marked it all down.

Having passed through much suffering, the Apostle Paul was still able to say, "For I reckon that the sufferings of this present time are not worthy to be compared with the glory which shall be revealed in us" (Rom. 8:18). This was the testimony of one who had suffered as few ever have.

Part of what Paul suffered is recorded in II Corinthians 11:24-28: "Of the Jews five times received I forty stripes save one. Thrice was I beaten with rods, once was I stoned, thrice I suffered shipwreck, a night and a day I have been in the deep; In journeyings often, in perils of waters, in perils of robbers, in perils by mine own countrymen, in perils by the heathen, in perils in the city, in perils in the wilderness, in perils in the sea, in perils among false brethren; In weariness and painfulness, in watchings often, in hunger and thirst, in fastings often, in cold and nakedness. Beside those things that are without, that which cometh upon me daily, the care of all the churches." Yet, Paul was able to say that the sufferings of the present time are not worthy to be compared with the glory which will be revealed in us.

The reason Paul was able to bear up under his suffering was that he realized it was temporary. He referred to this when he spoke of the sufferings of the "present time" (Rom. 8:18). He knew that suffering had only to do with his time on earth. Those who reject Jesus Christ as Saviour, however, will suffer throughout eternity. But those who have received Christ have already had the penalty of their sins paid and any suffering they endure will only be in this life.

Paul's reference to "the glory which shall be revealed in us" has to do with that which is eternal. The glory will be forever and ever. It has been revealed *unto* us now as we have met Christ, but then it will be revealed *in* us when we will have glorified bodies after the resurrection. Paul referred to our glorified bodies when he said, "Our conversation [citizenship] is in heaven; from whence also we look for the Saviour, the Lord Jesus Christ: Who shall change our vile body, that it may be fashioned like unto his glorious body, according to the working whereby he is able even to subdue all things unto himself" (Phil. 3:20,21).

Our glorified bodies will be part of the glory that will be revealed in us in eternity. If you are crippled, blind, or in any way maimed, be assured that this is only for the present time and is not worthy to be compared with the glory that will follow.

Not only will we have a glorified body, but we will have transformed minds. Paul referred to this when he said, "For now we see through a glass, darkly; but then face to face: now I know in part; but then shall I know even as also I am known" (I Cor. 13:12). In eternity we will have full knowledge and will understand why it was necessary for us to pass through suffering.

The glory that will be revealed in us also includes Christlikeness. This is emphasized in Romans 8:29 which says, "For whom he did foreknow, he also did predestinate to be conformed to the image of his Son, that he might be the firstborn among many brethren." Our

69

future Christlikeness is also mentioned in I John 3:2: "Beloved, now are we the sons of God, and it doth not yet appear what we shall be: but we know that, when he shall appear, we shall be like him; for we shall see him as he is."

It is clear from the Scriptures that suffering will be compensated. Though we suffer in this life, there will be incomparable glory to follow. Suffering is temporal and will pass but the glory to follow is eternal. Suffering is earthly; glory is heavenly. It is impossible to compare the finite with the infinite. In other words, *one second of glory outweighs a lifetime of suffering*. Regardless of the suffering that any Christian is enduring, he can be full of joy by knowing that God will compensate his suffering with glory to follow. This glory will be so great that it cannot even be compared with the present suffering.

Thought: Affliction to the people of God is the pruning knife to the vine to prepare for a greater fruitfulness.

Chapter 8

The Ultimate Goal of Suffering

The Apostle Paul endured extreme suffering throughout his life, but he had his eyes set on the goal beyond rather than on the suffering. Paul said, "We are troubled on every side, yet not distressed; we are perplexed, but not in despair; Persecuted, but not forsaken; cast down, but not destroyed" (II Cor. 4:8,9). Because Paul had his eyes set on the glory that was beyond his suffering, he could also say, "For which cause we faint not; but though our outward man perish, yet the inward man is renewed day by day. For our light affliction, which is but for a moment, worketh for us a far more exceeding and eternal weight of glory; While we look not at the things which are seen, but at the things which are not seen: for the things which are seen are temporal; but the things which are not seen are eternal" (II Cor. 4:16-18).

This was Paul's attitude in the midst of his suffering. The outward man was perishing under all the suffering, but the inward man was being renewed day after day. To him, no matter what suffering he experienced, it was a "light affliction" because it was temporary and would result in a "far more exceeding and eternal weight of glory." His eyes were set on the glory to follow, not on the suffering and affliction he was experiencing in this life. What the suffering accomplished for Paul it can also accomplish for us. We must fix our spiritual eyes on eternal things, that which is not seen by the physical eye.

This was the ultimate goal in suffering for the Apostle Paul and it ought also to be our ultimate goal in suffering.

What does suffering accomplish for us? From Hebrews 12:10 we have learned that chastening is "for our profit, that we might be partakers of his holiness." This ought to be first in our lives—to be partakers of His holiness. The following verse is so important that it ought to be memorized by every Christian: "Now no chastening for the present seemeth to be joyous, but grievous: nevertheless afterward it yieldeth the peaceable fruit of righteousness unto them which are exercised thereby" (12:11). Notice the key word "afterward." The writer had in view that which is eternal and unseen rather than that which is temporal and seen. He was looking at future rewards, not at present suffering. The writer was possibly a man of great suffering—it is quite probable that the Apostle Paul was the writer of Hebrews. He was a university graduate and a prominent ecclesiastic, but he became a man of sorrow. However, instead of being defeated by his sorrows he looked to the future and rejoiced in the "afterward."

Paul testified, "Yea doubtless, and I count all things but loss for the excellency of the knowledge of Christ Jesus my Lord: for whom I have suffered the loss of all things, and do count them but dung, that I may win Christ, And be found in him, not having mine own righteousness, which is of the law, but that which is through the faith of Christ, the righteousness which is of God by faith" (Phil. 3:8,9). Notice why Paul counted all things but loss—that he might "win Christ." He was not trying to win Christ for salvation because he already had salvation. Instead, Paul was talking as a child of God and wanted to win Christ in the sense that he wanted to be conformed to the image of Christ.

Paul did not want to be found with righteousness which he could perform, but he wanted to be found with the righteousness "which is through the faith of Christ." Again, it does not seem that Paul was talking about a salvation righteousness because he already had that. It seems rather that he was talking about a righteousness which is to be given to us and worked out in us through the Person of Christ. This kind of righteousness is emphasized in Hebrews 13:21 where it is asked that the God of peace "make you perfect in every good work to do his will, working in you that which is wellpleasing in his sight, through Jesus Christ; to whom be glory for ever and ever. Amen."

The Apostle Paul wanted to be mature in Christ—he yearned to be like Christ. Is this your desire? If so, it is important for you to remember that suffering will be necessary, for suffering is given for the purpose of conforming us to the image of Christ.

Paul's Desire

Philippians 3:10 continues the words of the Apostle Paul who said, "That I may know him, and the power of his resurrection, and the fellowship of his sufferings, being made conformable unto his death." We all want the power of Christ's resurrection, but do we want the fellowship of His sufferings? Notice, however, that they go together. It is not possible to have the power of His resurrection without experiencing the fellowship of His sufferings. Suffering is the means by which we can know the power of Christ's resurrection. Suffering, this "light affliction," works for us and makes us like Jesus Christ. We will be like Him in the resurrection but even now on this earth we can begin to know something about the power of His resurrection.

How can we be made conformable unto His death? Philippians 2:5-8 gives us the answer: "Let this mind be in you, which was also in Christ Jesus: Who, being in the form of God, thought it not robbery to be equal with God: But made himself of no reputation, and took upon him the form of a servant, and was made in the likeness of men: And being found in fashion as a man, he humbled himself, and became obedient unto death, even the death of the cross." Christ was willing to temporarily set aside His heavenly life. He gladly gave up His glory with the Father and veiled it temporarily for the sake of becoming a man in order to suffer and die on the cross for the sins of the world. Had He not done this, none of us would have been able to escape condemnation. In the light of Christ's humility and unselfishness, the

Apostle Paul said, "Let this mind be in you, which was also in Christ Jesus."

The one who has the mind of Christ will deny himself and submit to God. Christ Himself said, "If any man will come after me, let him deny himself, and take up his cross daily, and follow me" (Luke 9:23). This was Paul's attitude as evidenced by his words in Philippians 2:12-14: "Wherefore, my beloved, as ye have always obeyed, not as in my presence only, but now much more in my absence, work out your own salvation with fear and trembling. For it is God which worketh in you both to will and to do of his good pleasure. Do all things without murmurings and disputings." Paul erased from his mind the sufferings of the past and set his eyes on the future. Although the future might include more suffering, Paul was willing to accept it because it would make him more like Jesus Christ. The "high calling of God in Christ Jesus" is our calling to be like Jesus Christ.

Do you desire what the Apostle Paul desired? Do you really want to know the power of Christ's resurrection? Do you want to know the fullness of His indwelling? Do you want to be conformed to His image? Then accept the teaching of the Scriptures that maturity and conformity to the image of Christ come through suffering. Jacob experienced this when the Lord touched his thigh and caused him to suffer the rest of his life so he would remember that he was a Jacob in the flesh, but a spiritual giant with the Lord. Paul also experienced the truth of maturity through suffering inasmuch as the Lord gave him a thorn in the flesh that he might realize his weakness and walk in dependency on the Lord.

Many years ago when I was in Bible school, I met a man who was totally crippled except for his right arm and one of his fingers. When I went to visit this man I found him lying on his bed, propped up with a typewriter on his lap. With one finger he was laboriously pecking out some kind of message. He could not even move the typewriter carriage when he finished a line. He had a brother who was also crippled but was able to get around a little on his feet. This brother would move the carriage back every time it was needed. But the man who typed with one finger was joyous even though he suffered greatly. He even taught in college. He could not go there so the students came to his room. He spoke words of joy to my heart such as no other man has. This man and his crippled brother were cared for by their elderly mother. Within the week that this man was taken home to heaven, his mother and brother also died. They were not needed anymore.

When our eyes are set on the glory that is to follow we also can have joyous hearts in the midst of severe suffering.

There is also our own Eugene Clark. Many of you have heard about him and have faithfully prayed for him. Few people are suffering as this man is suffering. But in spite of his physical condition he continues to write a great deal of music—much of which is used by Back to the Bible. Out of the depths of his suffering he wrote the song *Nothing Is Impossible*. It has been multiplied into more than a million copies and is being sung all around the world. But we should not forget that it came out of suffering.

Do you want to be conformed to the image of Christ? If so, it will be necessary for God to allow you to suffer.

Romans 8:28-30

The ultimate goal of suffering is seen in Romans 8:28-30: "And we know that all things work together for good to them that love God, to them who are the called according to his purpose. For whom he did foreknow, he also did predestinate to be conformed to the image of his Son, that he might be the firstborn among many brethren. Moreover whom he did predestinate, them he also called: and whom he called, them he also justified: and whom he justified, them he also glorified."

Genesis 1 tells us how man was created in the image of God. However, the record of how that image was lost when sin entered is found in Genesis 3. Adam and Eve saw themselves naked, and the glory of God was gone. They became separated from God and He had to drive them out of the garden. In His grace, however, God made a way of atonement for them. But there is more; that is, through suffering, chastisement, and joyful submission on our part it is possible for that image to be restored. First, spiritual regeneration is necessary. Then, the molding process begins whereby we are conformed to the image of Christ. Therefore, the adversities of life—trials, troubles, sorrows, losses, suffering, pain, disappointments— all work for us. We are told this in II Corinthians

4:17: "For our light affliction, which is but for a moment, worketh for us a far more exceeding and eternal weight of glory." They work for us because it is through these things that we are conformed to the image of Christ. All of these are involved in the "all things" of Romans 8:28.

Paul said, "We know. . . ." He was not guessing; it was a matter of certainty. He also emphasized that "all things" are involved in what he was referring to. This includes the things we worry about, things that upset us, and heartaches and tests that come until we do not know which way to turn. These are the things the Apostle Paul was talking about. He said they "work together. . . ." These are important words. At the time we are enduring suffering it does not seem that it is the right thing for us. Sometimes we wonder why God allows such things to come into our lives. But remember the "afterward" of Hebrews 12:11. Keep in mind that during this life we may never see why a certain thing has any value for us. It is like putting a puzzle together. All the pieces must be put together before the puzzle is solved. One piece has no meaning by itself, but when all the pieces are put together the puzzle is solved. So also it takes all things working together in our lives to make us what God wants us to be.

Notice that all things work together "for good." We immediately see this as a wonderful truth. We want everything that is good. We do not care for anything that is bad or that brings disappointment. If we have a fine crop, that is good. If we have crop failure, that is bad. But in God's sight the failure may be good too. You may lose your job and consider that bad, but in God's sight it is good if it fits into His will for you. God knows what He is doing. The good that Paul emphasized is not only our good but also God's good. Whatever is for our good will also be for His good, for we are His children. Thus we rejoice together in Him, and He in us.

Are you qualified to claim the promise of Romans 8:28? Many claim this promise who have no right to do so. To whom is the promise made? Is it made to everybody? Please note that "all things work together for good to them that love God." The Greek tense of the word "love" emphasizes continuous action. It refers to the person who continually loves God. Notice another qualification is that this is only true "to them who are the called according to his purpose." These, then, are the two qualifications which must be met before we can say this verse applies to us. Only when we have met the qualifications can we claim the promise of this verse.

The First Qualification

Let us consider these qualifications in further detail. The first qualification is that we must love God. We cannot love God apart from the love that is planted in our hearts by the Holy Spirit; so, in a sense, all true Christians love Him. But I believe that this word "love" has a deeper meaning than that. Concerning some believers Revelation 2:4 says, "Thou hast left thy first love." From this we see it is possible to leave the love that we have for Him. Do you love Him enough to fellowship with Him through every kind of circumstance—even suffering? Do trials and tests bring you closer to Him?

We Christians sometimes give way to discouragement; we wonder why God makes us wait. For a long time I had been praying regarding certain things pertaining to the Back to the Bible Broadcast. Sometimes I had asked myself, "Why hasn't He done it? Why am I still having to wait?" Then one morning I read Isaiah 30:18: "Therefore will the Lord wait, that he may be gracious unto you, and therefore will he be exalted, that he may have mercy upon you: for the Lord is a God of judgment: blessed are all they that wait for him."

Sometimes God waits to answer our prayers so we will wait on Him. He waits that He may be gracious to us. Sometimes His waiting causes us to wait more upon Him and to be more appreciative when we finally see the answer to our prayers. If God answers our prayer immediately, perhaps we would soon forget it. He allows some things to be impressed on our hearts so we will not soon forget His goodness.

Think of Job and of how God permitted him to be pressed from every side. He even permitted Job's friends to visit him and to ridicule him. But Job waited. Finally he came to a full realization of his condition, and then God blessed him and showed him His mercy. In the Book of Job we find one of the greatest records of how God showed His grace to a man who had waited—possibly for years—in a condition of severe suffering. Perhaps you will wait for certain things until you enter into His presence, but if you really love Him you will gladly continue to wait on Him.

The Second Qualification

The second qualification is disclosed in the words "to them who are the called according to his purpose." God has a purpose for you, and He has called you. The message of this verse is for you if you are following His call because He wants to make you more fit for your particular place. A square peg does not fit into a round hole. God may have to whittle you down for a while to get you to fit the place for which He was called you.

Do not question how He is going to do it. That is not necessary for you or anyone else to know. The fact that He will do it should give you continual hope—even joy—in waiting on God.

The Purpose

Finally, God gives us the purpose for all of this: "For whom he did foreknow, he also did predestinate to be conformed to the image of his Son." Predestination is not hard to understand. Literally, it means that He has undertaken to see to it that you will be conformed to the image of His Son; that is, that you will be made like Him. "Beloved, now are we the sons of God, and it doth not yet appear what we shall be: but we know that, when he shall appear, we shall be like him; for we shall see him as he is" (I John 3:2). The more you rebel, the more you object, the more you walk after the flesh, the harder God will have to deal with you.

Also, in Romans 8:17 Paul said that we are "heirs of God, and joint-heirs with Christ; if so be that we suffer with him, that we may be also glorified together"—that we might have the same glory with Him.

There will be suffering, but Paul was not discouraged over this possibility. He said, "I reckon that the sufferings of this present time [this present life] are not worthy to be compared with the glory which shall be revealed in us" (Rom. 8:18).

Some time ago I stood in the Black Hills of South Dakota and looked up at the stone faces of four former presidents of the United States which were hewn out of a great mountain of granite. If those rocks were alive and could speak, they would tell of the pain which they went through during the chiseling, the blasting, and everything that had to be done to them. Tons and tons of rock had to be cleared away so that the likenesses of the four men could be brought out.

It may be that you and I are as hard as granite to work with, which means that the sufferings will be that much harder also. If you are a child of God, He has given you joy and the desire to fulfill His will and to live a victorious life. Only remember that He will have to chisel away a lot of things in your life until you are conformed to the image of His Son.

We are waiting for the future. God has given us an indication of what that future in Christ Jesus will be. Many Christians understand only that they are saved—they know hardly anything more. He has given us a foretaste of the power of the Godhead in us that we might be victorious over the things of this life. The more we desire the things of the Lord and the more we walk after the Spirit, the more we will realize what a wonderful life we have in Christ. We have the foretaste, but we are looking for the consummation in the future. We are groaning within ourselves now and waiting until we are placed at God's side as His sons with glorified bodies. Then we shall truly be like the Lord Jesus Christ. Hallelujah! What a wonderful Saviour!

"Being confident of this very thing, that he which hath begun a good work in [not "through" but "in"] you will perform it until the day of Jesus Christ" (Phil. 1:6).

Thought: How can the world know what Christ is like until we show what Christ can make us like?

...
...

Chapter 9

Our Attitude Toward Suffering

We must have the proper attitude toward suffering if we are to benefit from it. Hebrews 12:11 tells us, "Now no chastening for the present seemeth to be joyous, but grievous: nevertheless afterward [remember this key word] it yieldeth the peaceable fruit of righteousness unto them which are exercised thereby."

This promise is not to everyone, but only to those who are " exercised thereby." These are they who have been trained by what they have suffered; that is, they have been "trained thereby." This promise is not only to those who have suffered, but to those who have suffered with a right attitude so that it becomes a spiritual exercise. If the attitude is wrong, there will be no good fruit resulting from suffering. When the attitude is right, suffering becomes a spiritual exercise. To be "exercised thereby" is to be "spiritually exercised."

Hebrews 12 gives us many instructions about what our attitude should be in suffering. Before we consider what our attitude ought to be, let us consider what it ought not to be. Verse 5 in this chapter tells us, "And ye have forgotten the exhortation which speaketh unto you as unto children, My son, despise not thou the chastening of the Lord, nor faint when thou art rebuked of him." Here the command is clear that we are to despise not and to faint not.

Despising and fainting are two entirely different dangers that we are warned against. They are opposites. A person may become haughty and try to laugh off the rod of affliction; that is, he may have a stubborn will and refuse to be humbled by his afflictions. Or, he may faint and utterly sink beneath the load and give way to despair.

Despising the Chastening

There are many ways in which we may be guilty of despising God's chastening, but let us consider four of them in particular.

By Becoming Calloused

It is possible to despise God's chastening by becoming calloused to it. The world can produce only carnal wisdom which tells us, "Grit your teeth and make the best of it." That is the way the world looks at suffering, but to take such an attitude is to become calloused to it. For a Christian, to defy the adversities that aid growth in the Christian life is to despise chastening. Instead of hardening oneself against chastening, there should be a melting of the heart toward it. Regardless of what the Lord brings into your life to chasten you, do not harden yourself against it or become calloused to it. Do not respond by saying, "Well, if it has to be, then it has to be and I can't do anything about it. I will accept it and continue to suffer." No. Let God

85

melt your heart and speak to you through your affliction.

By Complaining

Another way we can despise chastening is by complaining. The Bible calls it "murmuring." There was much murmuring in the camp of Israel during their time in the wilderness. The Scriptures clearly show what God thinks about the murmuring of His children. Numbers 14 tells us, "And all the congregation lifted up their voice, and cried; and the people wept that night. And all the children of Israel murmured against Moses and against Aaron: and the whole congregation said unto them, Would God that we had died in the land of Egypt! or would God we had died in this wilderness!" (vv. 1,2). Later in this same chapter God told the Israelites, "Because all those men which have seen my glory, and my miracles, which I did in Egypt and in the wilderness, and have tempted me now these ten times, and have not hearkened to my voice: Surely they shall not see the land which I sware unto their fathers, neither shall any of them that provoked me see it." In other words, God told them, "I have been attempting to train you and prepare you to go in and to take the land, but what have you done? You have hardened your hearts; you have not hearkened to My voice." Because they would not heed what God was trying to do in their lives, God refused to let them enter the land.

In verse 27 of this chapter God spoke to Moses and Aaron and said, "How long shall I bear with this evil congregation, which murmur against me? I have heard the murmurings of the children of Israel, which they murmur against me." Then God instructed Moses and Aaron to say to the Israelites, "Your carcases shall fall in this wilderness; and all that were numbered of you, according to your whole number, from twenty years old and upward, which have murmured against me" (v. 29). This shows us how much God hates murmuring or complaining.

The children of Israel had come to a place called Kadesh-barnea and there they had to make a decision whether to go into the land or not. At Kadesh-barnea they had sent 12 spies into the land and 10 had come back saying, in effect, "It cannot be done, it cannot be done." The Israelites now felt they had come to the end of their rope, for they did not understand God's testings. The things around them were too great for them—the walls were too tall and the giants were too big. God was chastening, or testing, the Israelites but they murmured against Him. Because of this murmuring they were not able to enter the Promised Land. They were willing to believe God to come out of Egypt, but they did not have the faith to enter into their rest. Therefore, though they were redeemed, they brought 40 years of grief to God their Father.

We also see how deadly complaining and murmuring can be as we read Psalm 106. Referring again to the Israelites, the Word of God says, "Yea, they despised the pleasant land, they believed not his word: But murmured in their tents, and hearkened not unto the voice of the Lord. Therefore he lifted up his hand against them, to overthrow them in the wilderness" (vv.24-26). God gave the Israelites only good, but they murmured against Him and as a result they missed inheriting the land. The land symbolizes the pleasant and fruitful life and the place for mature Christian living.

Have you missed what God has for you because you have taken a wrong attitude toward God's testings and chastenings? Have you murmured and complained instead of humbling yourself before God and letting Him speak to you? How quickly we begin to complain when afflictions come! Hardly has the first affliction come when we begin to ask, "Why did this happen to me? If God really loves me why did He permit it?"

Having seen the negative aspect—that we are to despise not and to faint not in the midst of suffering—Psalm 37 gives us the positive aspect of this truth. Verses 4 and 5 tell us, "Delight thyself also in the Lord; and he shall give thee the desires of thine heart. Commit thy way unto the Lord; trust also in him; and he shall bring it to pass." Here we are told to rest in the Lord and wait patiently for Him. We are not to fret ourselves because of the man who prospers in his way or because of the man who brings wicked devices to pass. Beware! It goes hard for murmurers. Therefore, God warns each of His children: "My son, despise not thou the chastening of the Lord."

By Criticism

A third way that we can despise the chastening of the Lord is by criticism; that is, questioning the usefulness of the chastising. The word "despise" means to "make light of." Such a person thinks the chastening is useless and he makes light of it by questioning its value. Such Christians forget that

God is working all things together for good to them that love Him and who are called according to His purpose, until they be conformed to the image of His Son (Rom. 8:28,29). Such Christians also need to remember the potter and the clay. Does the clay have any right to say to the potter, "Why hast thou made me thus"? (Rom. 9:20). Instead of an attitude like this, we should humble ourselves before the Lord and realize that His chastening can profit us greatly.

Perhaps someone says, "If I just had good health, I would attend the regular church meetings more often." Let me ask you, How regularly did you attend them when you were well? Or someone may say, "If I did not have all of these business reverses, I would give God more for His work." But are you giving what you can even now?

Are we questioning God's chastening in our lives? If so, we are despising the chastening by criticism.

Too often we, like Jacob, say, "All these things are against me" (Gen. 42:36). These were Jacob's words after Joseph had been sold into Egypt and now the brothers were wanting to take Benjamin down also so they could get food. But we must realize that God never works against us—He always works for our good. Shall our ignorance challenge God's wisdom? Shall our shortsightedness challenge omniscience?

Fanny Crosby was blind all 95 years of her life, but she was a victorious Christian and wrote hundreds of songs. In spite of her physical condition she was able to write such a song as *To God Be the Glory*. How about you? What is your attitude toward suffering?

By Carelessness

Another way that we can despise the chastening of the Lord is by carelessness. By being careless to correct our ways we are actually despising the chastening of the Lord. God has allowed the rod for our correction, but it is all in vain if we refuse to learn. It is possible for sickness, reverses and bereavement to come into our lives without our prayerfully examining ourselves or seeking God's desire for our lives. Be assured that there is always a reason for God's chastening. In fact, we can often avoid more chastening by diligently seeking God's reason for it. James indicated this when he wrote, "My brethren, count it all joy when ye fall into divers temptations; Knowing this, that the trying of your faith worketh patience" (1:2,3). Verse 5 in this chapter tells every Christian, "If any of you lack wisdom, let him ask of God, that giveth to all men liberally, and upbraideth not; and it shall be given him."

If you lack wisdom as to why God has allowed chastening to come into your life, then ask Him. He will not upbraid you or scold you but rather He will give you wisdom about these matters. Verse 5 is often used out of context but its primary meaning is that when you are suffering and do not know why, ask God and He will give you the answer.

Many years ago I received a long-distance telephone call from a dear friend. This friend told of a very serious accident that happened in their family. The friend asked me to pray with them about four things and one of them was: "That God will show us what He wants to teach us through this serious lesson." Because they prayed for such wisdom, God gave them the answer and they corrected their ways accordingly.

God may be speaking to you in just the same way today. Have you gone to Him in prayer to see why He has had to bring chastening into your life? Do you have a good attitude toward the chastening of the Lord because it is your sincere desire to be conformed to the image of Christ?

Faint Not

Christians are not to faint under the pressure of the chastening of God. We are not to give way to despair. In I Corinthians 10:13 God has promised that "there hath no temptation taken you but such as is common to man: but God is faithful, who will not suffer you to be tempted above that ye are able; but will with the temptation also make a way to escape, that ye may be able to bear it." God did not say that He would take the testing away but He did promise that we would not be tested beyond our ability to bear it. He puts at our disposal all the grace we need and provides an escape that we may be able to bear the testing.

By Giving Up

There are different ways that a Christian can faint under the pressure of chastening. One way is when he gives up all efforts to win. Perhaps he says in hopelessness, "Well, what's the use? I just can't take it anymore." Then he sinks into despondency and concludes that his testing is more than he can possibly endure. He does not cast himself on the grace of God; instead, his heart fails him. The voice

91

of thanksgiving is silent, rather than thanking God for what He is allowing and saying, "Lord, I know You are doing it for my good, and I appropriate by faith and accept the strength to be able to bear up under this thing." When a Christian faints in the spiritual battle, he renders himself unfit for the discharge of his duties. When a person faints physically, he loses consciousness and becomes motionless. Many Christians seem also to be this way—they are not aware of what God is doing for them because they have spiritually fainted and given up the fight.

The day I was baptized the pastor gave each one of us a special verse. The one he gave me has stuck with me all these years. The verse is I Timothy 6:12: "Fight the good fight of faith." In the Apostle Paul's second letter to Timothy he said of himself, "I have fought a good fight, I have finished my course, I have kept the faith" (4:7).

Paul was not talking about a physical fight but rather a spiritual fight. It was not a fight of the flesh but the fight of faith. If anyone was harrassed and under spiritual trials and affliction, it was the Apostle Paul. But he fought through to victory. By faith he accepted his trials and pushed on for God.

In I Thessalonians 4:13 the Apostle Paul told us, "Sorrow not, even as others which have no hope." Here he was speaking about those who had lost loved ones through death. If the one who died was a believer, then we are not to sorrow as those who have no hope. But death is just one of the afflictions that come to us and this same principle can be applied to our other suffering. We are not to sorrow in our suffering as those who have no hope because we Christians are able to see beyond the suffering. We have hope because we know these tribulations will bring forth righteousness as we are exercised thereby. The result of the suffering is that we will be conformed to the image of God's Son, Jesus Christ. Therefore, we are not to faint when we are rebuked of the Lord.

In Galatians 6:9 we are told, "Let us not be weary in well doing: for in due season [not always right away], we shall reap, if we faint not." Most of this reaping will be in eternity for we will receive our rewards when Christ comes to take us to Himself. We shall reap *then* if we do not faint *now*. But if we faint under the load now, there will be no reaping then.

The matter of fainting is also mentioned in Luke 18:1 which records the words of Christ who said, "Men ought always to pray, and not to faint." We are not to faint, but we are to go to Him in prayer even as James said that those who lack wisdom should ask of God.

Then there is Isaiah 40:31 which says, "But they that wait upon the Lord shall renew their strength; they shall mount up with wings as eagles; they shall run, and not be weary; and they shall walk, and not faint." The word "wait" means "to expect" or "to look for." Here we see a hope that is solidly placed in the Lord. To whom is this promise given? It is given to the ones who expectantly wait on the Lord for what He has for them. Because they are waiting expectantly on the Lord, they shall not faint.

Jesus Himself is a wonderful example of this truth. Hebrews 12:2 reminds us that as we run with patience the race that is set before us, we are to be constantly "looking unto Jesus the author

93

and finisher of our faith; who for the joy that was set before him endured the cross, despising the shame, and is set down at the right hand of the throne of God." Christ was willing to endure the cross because of the joy that was set before Him. He wanted to have you and me as His children forever. This was His joy. He despised the shame of the cross, but He wanted the joy of our becoming His children and He had to pay the penalty for our sins for this to be possible. Verse 3 of this chapter encourages us to remember Christ's example when it says, "For consider him that endured such contradiction of sinners against himself, lest ye be wearied and faint in your minds."

We are to go to the Lord and be reminded of all that He went through for us. We should consider Him as He stood before Pilate—the crown of thorns, the whippings, the scourgings, the misrepresentation and the false accusations. When we remember these things about Christ, we will not faint in our minds regarding our own trials. He is our example. He passed through His trials victoriously and now He indwells us and is our strength as we depend on Him. Christ is our life, as we are told in Colossians 1:27: "Christ in you, the hope of glory."

By Questioning Sonship

Christians also faint when they question their sonship; that is, when afflictions cause them to doubt their salvation. Some may think that because they are children of God they should not be experiencing afflictions, so when afflictions come they doubt their salvation. However, the Scriptures are clear about the righteous suffering affliction. The psalmist said, "Many are the afflictions of the righteous: but the Lord delivereth him out of them all" (34:19). Acts 14:22 also indicates the affliction of the righteous: "We must through much tribulation enter into the kingdom of God." Second Timothy 3:12 verifies this same truth: "Yea, and all that will live godly in Christ Jesus shall suffer persecution."

What is meant by living "godly in Christ Jesus"? If you are living according to the law and trying to do good, you may not suffer much persecution from other people. But when you take a stand for Jesus Christ and declare that He is in you and that you are living by His strength, you will suffer persecution because people will not understand. They will not be able to comprehend this spiritual truth. However, remember the words of Christ: "In the world ye shall have tribulation; but be of good cheer; I have overcome the world" (John 16:33).

John 15:2 also records the words of Christ who said, "Every branch in me that beareth not fruit he taketh away: and every branch that beareth fruit, he purgeth it, that it may bring forth more fruit." Are you a branch that does not bear fruit? Are you one who is always complaining and fainting under affliction? Beware. Such a person will be taken away; that is, he will be set aside or set on the shelf. Are you a fruitbearing branch? Through affliction God will make it possible for you to bear even more fruit. This is what God is trying to accomplish in our lives and we need to keep our eyes on Him.

Those who doubt that chastening should come to Christians need to be reminded of Hebrews

12:7,8: "If ye endure chastening, God dealeth with you as with sons; for what son is he whom the father chasteneth not? But if ye be without chastisement, whereof all are partakers, then are ye bastards, and not sons." To "endure chastening" means more than just suffering through it; it means to have the joy of God in the midst of suffering. As we see from these verses, if you are not chastened then you have reason to question whether you are really a Christian. When you receive Jesus Christ as Saviour, God then deals with you as a son. This in itself should encourage us so that we endure chastening with joy.

In verse 9 of this same passage we see that we are to put ourselves in subjection to God. Here we are told, "Furthermore we have had fathers of our flesh which corrected us, and we gave them reverence: shall we not much rather be in subjection unto the Father of spirits, and live?" A true father concerns himself with the welfare of his family and this includes discipline and correction. However, he does not do this to outsiders. The fact that we are being chastened shows God is treating us as sons because we have received Jesus Christ as Saviour. Therefore, when we suffer affliction let us say, "Thank You, Lord. Now I know that You love me, and because You love me as a son, You deal with me as a son."

By Despairing

Christians also faint when they despair. God says that we should endure, but some feel that they may never get out from under their affliction even though they may have prayed for years about it. It seems the clouds are never lifted. Some even say, "I have pleaded His promises but things are absolutely no better. I have called on Him, but He has not delivered me."

Let us examine this further. What does God mean when He promises to "deliver" us? In Psalm 91:15 God says, "He shall call upon me, and I will answer him: I will be with him in trouble; I will deliver him, and honour him." Psalm 50:15 tells us the same thing: "Call upon me in the day of trouble: I will deliver thee, and thou shalt glorify me." What is meant by God's promise to deliver us?

The root word for "deliver" can have the meaning of "to equip" or "to arm" in the sense of preparing for battle. Thus we see that God strengthens us and arms us as soldiers. He will not allow us to be tempted above what we are able to bear, but with the temptation He will make a way to escape so we will be able to bear it. God will arm us for the spiritual battle so we may be able to bear our trials. It does not mean that He will necessarily deliver us from the trial, but rather that He will strengthen us so we may be able to bear it.

How to Suffer as a Christian

The First Epistle of Peter particularly emphasizes suffering. Peter's letter tells us of the attitude that Christians should have in an unfriendly world. Peter wrote: "Yet if any man suffer as a Christian, let him not be ashamed; but let him glorify God on this behalf" (I Pet. 4:16).

The Christian attitude is the realization that we live in an unfriendly world but that we are only pilgrims and strangers here, looking forward to our

97

home in heaven. Old Testament men such as Abraham, Isaac and Jacob lived in tents even though they were rich as far as the world's standards were concerned. They suffered a great deal but they lived as strangers and pilgrims in this world. This is what we are also. We are not immune from the suffering of the world just because we are Christians.

What does it mean to suffer as Christians? First, it means to suffer willingly. Whatever our lot is as Christians, we should willingly receive our chastening from the Lord. First Peter 4:16 tells us that those who suffer should not be ashamed but ought to glorify God. However, we are to suffer as Christians, not as evildoers. The preceding verse says, "But let none of you suffer as a murderer, or as a thief, or as an evildoer, or as a busybody in other men's matters." We ought not to be guilty of these sins which bring on suffering. The mark of the true Christian is that he suffers for the good he does and yet he has a good attitude toward the Lord regarding the suffering. No one needs to be ashamed if he suffers as a Christian. Jesus Christ Himself warned, "In the world ye shall have tribulation: but be of good cheer; I have overcome the world" (John 16:33). The Apostle Paul said that everyone who "will live godly in Christ Jesus shall suffer persecution" (II Tim. 3:12).

In contrast to those who suffer as Christians, there are those who suffer for doing evil. In I Peter 4:14 the apostle referred to both groups when he said, "If ye be reproached for the name of Christ, happy are ye; for the spirit of glory and of God resteth upon you: on their part he is evil spoken of, but on your part he is glorified." There are those who will ridicule you because you are a Christian. They will say, "See, you say you are a Christian and yet you have to suffer more than we do." On their part Christ is "evil spoken of," but, when we suffer for Him, on our part "he is glorified." It is our responsibility, therefore, to display the attitude towards suffering that is becoming to a Christian. A person has nothing to be ashamed of when he suffers as a result of being a Christian.

Uncomplainingly

Perhaps you ask, How do we suffer as Christians? We should suffer without complaining. Instead, we should thank the Lord for what He is doing in and through us. When we turn to God's Word and encourage ourselves by the Scriptures, we will become thankful for all that God is doing on our behalf. We will be thankful for God's promise that He will not permit us to suffer beyond what we are able to bear (I Cor. 10:13). We will also be thankful for the reminder of II Corinthians 9:8: "God is able to make all grace abound toward you; that ye, always having all sufficiency in all things, may abound to every good work." This also is a verse you should memorize. I memorized it many years ago and have found it to be of much encouragement.

Unresistingly

In suffering as Christians, we should suffer without resisting. First Peter 4:19 tells us, "Wherefore let them that suffer according to the will of God commit the keeping of their souls to him in well doing, as unto a faithful Creator." You need to commit the keeping of your soul to God so that He will keep you doing well in spite of suffering. He is a faithful Creator; therefore, He can always be counted on. We must see that He has loving wisdom and will not test us beyond our ability.

When we suffer according to the will of God we need the reminder of Hebrews 10:36: "For ye have need of patience, that, after ye have done the will of God, ye might receive the promise." God's purpose for permitting the Christian to suffer is stated in I Peter 5:10: "But the God of all grace, who hath called us unto his eternal glory by Christ Jesus, after that ye have suffered a while, make you perfect, stablish, strengthen, settle you." It is the will of God that we have a certain amount of affliction so that this will draw us into an even better relationship with Him. A constant yielding to Him will result in much fruit.

Psalm 37:5 also refers to the patience and confidence we need in God when it says, "Commit thy way unto the Lord; trust also in him; and he shall bring it to pass." Over 30 years ago the Lord brought this verse to my attention in a special way. I claimed the promise of this verse then and it has been of much spiritual comfort to me through the years.

Undeservedly

Suffering as Christians means that we should not be suffering for wrongdoing. Others may mistreat us and we will suffer without just cause, but we should not be guilty of doing wrong which

100

deserves suffering. First Peter 2:19,20 says, "For this is thankworthy, if a man for conscience toward God endure grief, suffering wrongfully. For what glory is it, if, when ye be buffeted for your faults, ye shall take it patiently? but if, when ye do well, and suffer for it, ye take it patiently, this is acceptable with God." It is "thankworthy" in that God gives us grace. Oh, that we might see how precious it is in God's sight when we suffer for doing good.

This same thought is emphasized in I Peter 3:14-17: "But and if ye suffer for righteousness' sake, happy are ye: and be not afraid of their terror, neither be troubled; But sanctify the Lord God in your hearts: and be ready always to give an answer to every man that asketh you a reason of the hope that is in you with meekness and fear: Having a good conscience; that, whereas they speak evil of you, as of evildoers, they may be ashamed that falsely accuse your good conversation in Christ. For it is better, if the will of God be so, that ye suffer for well doing, than for evil doing."

We sanctify the Lord God in our hearts by setting Him apart in our hearts and saying, "Lord, I am going to stay with You and do Your will. I know when You are through with me I shall come forth as gold." We are to be ready to give an answer so that others might see that in spite of our suffering we have something they do not have. Always be ready to tell others what you have—the Lord Jesus Christ. We are to so live that unbelievers will be ashamed of accusing us. When you have difficulty having the right attitude toward suffering, read I Peter over and over again.

101

With and for Christ

Christ is our example as to what our attitude should be toward suffering. Because He lives within every Christian, He is more than an example. He lives in Christians to again produce the same kind of life which He lived while on earth. As we permit Him to live His life in us we become conformed to His image. We are told about Christ's example in I Peter 2:21-24: "For even hereunto were ye called: because Christ also suffered for us, leaving us an example, that ye should follow his steps: Who did no sin, neither was guile found in his mouth: Who, when he was reviled, reviled not again; when he suffered, he threatened not; but committed himself to him that judgeth righteously: Who his own self bare our sins in his own body on the tree, that we, being dead to sins, should live unto righteousness: by whose stripes ye were healed."

First Peter 3:18 tells us the purpose of Christ's suffering: "For Christ also hath once suffered for sins, the just for the unjust, that he might bring us to God, being put to death in the flesh, but quickened by the Spirit."

We who know Jesus Christ as Saviour should willingly suffer not only with Him, but also for Him because of all He has done for us. The Scriptures urge us to "go forth therefore unto him without the camp, bearing his reproach" (Heb. 13:13).

The Apostle Paul suffered many things and he said that he was "always bearing about in the body the dying of the Lord Jesus, that the life also of Jesus might be made manifest in our body. For we which live are alway delivered unto death for Jesus' sake, that the life also of Jesus might be made manifest in our mortal flesh" (II Cor. 4:10,11). This was the kind of life the Apostle Paul constantly lived. He urged others on for Christ when he said, "We then, as workers together with him, beseech you also that ye receive not the grace of God in vain" (II Cor. 6:1). When we yield to Christ and let Him live out His life through us, we will live without blame.

In Philippians 1:29 Christians are told, "For unto you it is given in the behalf of Christ, not only to believe on him, but also to suffer for his sake."

Rejoicingly

Christians are to suffer rejoicingly for the Lord Jesus Christ. Chapter 5 of Acts records that the disciples were flogged and commanded not to teach anymore in the name of Christ. After they had been beaten "they departed from the presence of the council, rejoicing that they were counted worthy to suffer shame for his name" (v. 41). Peter told us how to react toward such suffering when he said, "Beloved, think it not strange concerning the fiery trial which is to try you, as though some strange thing happened unto you: But rejoice, inasmuch as ye are partakers of Christ's sufferings; that, when his glory shall be revealed, ye may be glad also with exceeding joy" (I Pet. 4:12,13).

According to the Will of God

We have already seen from I Peter 4:19 that our suffering ought to be according to the will of God. We need to commit everything to Him with

103

the confidence that He will see us through every trial.

We also need to remember Romans 8:28-30 which emphasizes that God will see us all the way through from beginning to end. Verse 30 says, "Moreover whom he did predestinate, them he also called: and whom he called, them he also justified: and whom he justified, them he also glorified."

The Apostle Paul illustrates the kind of confidence that we need to have in God even in the midst of suffering. In his last letter to Timothy, Paul told how he was suffering and urged Timothy: "Do thy diligence to come shortly unto me" (II Tim. 4:9). Demas had forsaken Paul because he loved the world more than fellowship with other Christians. Paul was in a dungeon and was suffering, especially from the dampness of the dungeon. He wrote Timothy, "The cloke that I left at Troas with Carpus, when thou comest, bring with thee" (v. 13). The need for this cloak was urgent as indicated by Paul's words, "Do thy diligence to come before winter" (v. 21). However, in the midst of his suffering Paul had confidence in the Lord. Paul said, "The Lord shall deliver me from every evil work, and will preserve me unto his heavenly kingdom: to whom be glory for ever and ever. Amen" (v. 18).

Before Timothy arrived in Rome the Apostle Paul had been beheaded. Yet Paul had said, "The Lord shall deliver me from every evil work." Was Paul mistaken? The answer lies in knowing what Paul meant when he referred to being delivered.

By using the word "deliver" Paul did not mean that God would necessarily take him out of the dungeon. But he had confidence in God that no matter how difficult the testing, God would make a way out which would enable him to be a testimony. Paul had confidence that God would deliver him from "every evil work." In other words, he was persuaded that God would not let him get an evil attitude about the trials he was enduring. Paul also had confidence that God would preserve him unto the "heavenly kingdom." Regardless of what the testing might be, Paul believed that the Lord was able to strengthen him for it and preserve him for the heavenly kingdom. When Paul thought of God's faithfulness in the midst of his trials he exclaimed: "To whom be glory for ever and ever. Amen."

In Psalm 91:14 God says, "Because he hath set his love upon me, therefore will I deliver him: I will set him on high, because he hath known my name." The word "deliver" in this verse emphasizes a way out or a rescue. However, in the following verse—Psalm 91:15—another word for "deliver" is used when it says, "He shall call upon me, and I will answer him: I will be with him in trouble; I will deliver him, and honour him." Here the word means "to draw out" or "to draw away." When this word is used in the passive voice it emphasizes an equipping or arming such as a soldier is armed for battle.

The word "escape" in I Corinthians 10:13 literally means "a way out." God always provides a means of escape for the Christian; that is, He always makes a way out so that the Christian is able to bear the testing. Thus we see that God does not always deliver us from the midst of testing but He does always strengthen and enable us so we are able to bear up under the testing. If God delivered us from the midst of testing, then His purpose in molding our lives into what He wants them to be—conformed to the image of Christ—could not be served.

Thought: Christian heroes have not emerged from brilliantly lighted halls of luxury and self-indulgence, but from the darkened byways of suffering and persecution.

Chapter 10

Exhortations and Practical Suggestions Concerning Suffering

Exhortations

Hebrews 12 gives us several exhortations concerning suffering. Verses 12 through 17 are especially meaningful in this regard. Verse 12 says, "Wherefore lift up the hands which hang down, and the feeble knees." That is, take a fresh grip on life. We need to brace our trembling limbs. God knows we have afflictions because He has permitted them and has a definite reason for them. His goal for the sufferings will only be accomplished as we "despise not" His chastening, "nor faint" when we are rebuked of Him (v. 5). We are also to "endure chastening" (v. 7) and subject ourselves to the Father (v. 9). When these things are true in our lives then God's purpose for suffering will be fully accomplished. We must see that the Lord is allowing the affliction and trust Him for grace to bear up under it.

There are some verses in I John 3 that are also of special comfort in this matter. The apostle said, "Behold, what manner of love the Father hath bestowed upon us, that we should be called the sons of God, therefore the world knoweth us not,

107

because it knew him not" (v. 1). We usually apply the truth of this verse to salvation because it tells of God's love being exercised toward us. However, the verse refers to much more than just salvation. It refers to our position as "sons of God"—those who are bearing up under what God is allowing to come into their lives.

In the light of this, verse 2 continues the thought, "Beloved, now are we the sons of God, and it doth not yet appear what we shall be: but we know that, when he shall appear, we shall be like him; for we shall see him as he is." That we are sons of God is a fact based on our decision to receive Jesus Christ as Saviour. This verse emphasizes that what God has begun in us He will continue until the day of Jesus Christ. He will see us through. He will bring things to bear in our lives that will be used to conform us to the image of His Son. The whole process is God's undertaking.

Having received Christ as Saviour we are the sons of God and He treats us as sons so we might become like Him. First John 3:3 shows the results of knowing these truths: "Every man that hath this hope in him purifieth himself, even as he is pure." The Christian braces up under the whole load and allows God to cleanse his life from the things that are wrong. Do you have this hope that God will see you through to the end—that He will conform you into the image of His dear Son? If so, then take a new hold on life and let God accomplish His purpose through you.

Straight Paths

Having exhorted us to "lift up the hands which hang down, and the feeble knees," the writer of

Hebrews continued, "and make straight paths for your feet, lest that which is lame be turned out of the way; but let it rather be healed" (12:13). The "straight paths" emphasizes the need for even-keel Christians. This is in contrast to those who are constantly experiencing peaks and valleys in their Christian lives. Rather than having balanced lives, they are either way up or way down. Such Christians are usually depending too much on circumstances. We must always remember that it is God who orders and controls the circumstances.

Paul's confidence in the Lord in controlling the circumstances is seen when he wrote to the Philippians after they had sent a gift to him. Paul wrote: "Not that I speak in respect of want: for I have learned, in whatsoever state I am, therewith to be content" (4:11). Notice that Paul said, "I have learned." Contentment in every kind of situation does not come easily for us and it did not come easily for the Apostle Paul. He had to learn to be content. It was suffering that taught him to be content regardless of his circumstances. Paul said, "I know both how to be abased, and I know how to abound: every where and in all things I am instructed both to be full and to be hungry, both to abound and to suffer need. I can do all things through Christ which strengtheneth me" (4:12,13). Paul thanked the Philippians for helping him in his need but he wanted them to know he was not complaining, because he had learned contentment in the Lord regardless of the circumstances. We too can learn the same thing.

Hebrews 12:13 refers to straight paths for the feet "lest that which is lame be turned out of the way; but let it rather be healed." Others are

109

affected by our behavior whether they are Christians or unbelievers. The way many of us act under difficult circumstances brings a reproach or mockery upon Christianity. So the writer of Hebrews urges Christians to make straight paths so others who are watching might take courage and follow the same Christ. Such a testimony will attract unbelievers to Christ and will also encourage weaker Christians. As they see your contentment in the midst of suffering they will wonder what you have that they do not have. This will give you opportunity to tell them about Christ. That which God gives or allows to come into our lives is for our purification so that we might not be an offense to those seeking to know Him.

Follow Peace and Holiness

Hebrews 12:14 exhorts: "Follow peace with all men, and holiness, without which no man shall see the Lord." We are to pursue peace. Ephesians 4:3 tells us we ought to be "endeavouring to keep the unity of the Spirit in the bond of peace." In other words, it is not a peace we have to work for, but a peace we are to keep. The Holy Spirit has produced this peace in our lives, and between one another, and it is our responsibility to keep it.

Hebrews 12:14 says also that we are to follow "holiness" as well as peace. "Holiness" means "consecration" or "set-apartness." The holiness which we receive when we are born again is an imputed holiness. God gives His righteousness to us so that positionally we are perfect in Him. This imputed holiness is seen in Hebrews 10:10: "By the which will we are sanctified through the offering of the body of Jesus Christ once for all." This is also emphasized in verse 14 of the same chapter where we are told, "For by one offering he hath perfected for ever them that are sanctified." This is imputed holiness which we have because of our position in Christ.

However, Hebrews 13 describes imparted holiness—that which God works out through our lives in our spiritual activity. This imparted holiness is referred to in Hebrews 13:20,21: "Now the God of peace . . . make you perfect in every good work to do his will, working in you that which is wellpleasing in his sight, through Jesus Christ; to whom be glory for ever and ever. Amen." Imparted holiness is also emphasized in Romans 12:1: "I beseech you therefore, brethren, by the mercies of God, that ye present your bodies a living sacrifice, holy, acceptable unto God, which is your reasonable service." This is spiritual activity resulting from the indwelling Christ's energy within us.

A Serious Admonition

Hebrews 12:15 has a very important admonition for every Christian: "Looking diligently lest any man fail of the grace of God; lest any root of bitterness springing up trouble you, and thereby many be defiled." No one need lack the grace of God because God's grace is sufficient for every need. Since God's grace is sufficient, we lack His grace only when we fail to appropriate it. Notice that when one fails to appropriate the grace of God, a root of bitterness springs up to trouble him. There is danger in failing to receive God's grace and it results in bitterness in our inner spirit. We appropriate His grace by faith. Let us come to the Lord and say, "Lord, I will accept Your grace which is sufficient for my every need."

In II Corinthians 9:8 we are assured that "God is able to make all grace abound toward you; that ye, always having all sufficiency in all things, may abound to every good work." The Apostle Paul experienced the sufficiency of God's grace. Although God would not remove Paul's thorn in the flesh, He assured him, "My grace is sufficient for thee: for my strength is made perfect in weakness" (II Cor. 12:9).

A dear aunt of mine, who now has been with the Lord many years, was bedridden for nearly 15 years of her life. During those years when we would visit her she would always be rejoicing in the Lord. She was always on top of the world. She had left word that when she died I was to preach her funeral sermon and that the text was to be II Corinthians 12:9: "My grace is sufficient for thee." She wanted everyone to know that the grace of God was sufficient for her. It was a joy to speak at her funeral because she lived such a godly life and was so fruitful even though she was bedridden.

If we do not appropriate the grace of God, a root of bitterness will spring up within us and this will poison the lives of others. However, a good spirit, as well as a bad spirit, is contagious. If you have the right attitude toward suffering by accepting God's sufficient grace for it, you will be a great encouragement to others. Obviously, you cannot work for grace. You simply appropriate it by saying, "Lord, I need Your grace and I will accept Your sufficient grace for today's trials."

The Book of Hebrews then gives us a very serious warning by way of illustration. We are told, "Lest there be any fornicator, or profane person, as Esau, who for one morsel of meat sold his birthright" (12:16). This refers to the incident recorded in Genesis 25:27-34. Esau was hungry and asked for some food but first Jacob asked Esau to sell him his birthright. Esau was so hungry that he sold his birthright to Jacob. For momentary fleshly gratification, Esau sold his birthright. The passage in Genesis 25 ends by saying, "Thus Esau despised his birthright." Esau gave up the spiritual privileges that would have been his because of his birthright. According to the Scriptures, the spiritual blessings were to come through Jacob but it was not necessary for him to go after the birthright the way he did or for Esau to despise it as he did.

Our birthright is Christ Himself as all Christians are told in Colossians 1:27: "Christ in you, the hope of glory." Because Christ indwelt the Apostle Paul, as He does every Christian, Paul wrote: "I can do all things through Christ which strengtheneth me" (Phil. 4:13).

Because Christ is our heritage, Colossians 2:6-8 tells us, "As ye have therefore received Christ Jesus the Lord, so walk ye in him: Rooted and built up in him, and stablished in the faith, as ye have been taught, abounding therein with thanksgiving. Beware lest any man spoil you through philosophy and vain deceit, after the tradition of men, after the rudiments of the world, and not after Christ." We receive Jesus Christ by faith and this is the way we are to walk in Him. When our trials and testings come we are to trust God for more grace. We are

113

not to have confidence in the world's philosophy and vain deceit which says, "Grit your teeth and bear your suffering." Our dependence is on the Lord, not on our own strength. Jesus Christ is able to give us all we need "for in him dwelleth all the fulness of the Godhead bodily" (Col. 2:9). Verse 10 continues by saying, "And ye are complete in him." Everything we need can be found in Jesus Christ, so let us trust Him for it.

Practical Suggestions

We must remember that the key to blessing is not the suffering itself, but suffering in the right attitude. There are some additional suggestions that may be of help to you when trials come. These suggestions will help you to be an even-keel Christian even though you are passing through adverse circumstances.

Renew Confidence in God

First, renew your confidence in God. You can renew your confidence in Him by reminding yourself of the many wonderful truths in the Word of God. Along with the Apostle Paul you should be able to say, "We know that all things work together for good to them that love God, to them who are the called according to his purpose" (Rom. 8:28).

Remember also that there are many afflictions for the believer but that God will deliver. Psalm 34:19 assures us that "many are the afflictions of the righteous: but the Lord delivereth him out of them all." As mentioned previously, the word

114

"deliver" not only has the meaning of "rescue" but also of "arming" or "equipping." The Lord will give you the strength to bear up under your trials. No matter how difficult the testing, God will make a way out which will enable you to bear it.

Renew your confidence in God by reminding yourself of His wonderful faithfulness. Lamentations 3:22,23 says, "It is of the Lord's mercies that we are not consumed, because his compassions fail not. They are new every morning: great is thy faithfulness." Bask yourself in God's faithfulness. He will not test you beyond what you are able to bear. He will enable you to bear it. Why? Because He is faithful to you.

Renew your confidence in God by turning to the Book of Isaiah and noting such verses as 41:13: "For I the Lord thy God will hold thy right hand, saying unto thee, Fear not; I will help thee." Notice also verses 3 and 4 of chapter 26: "Thou wilt keep him in perfect peace, whose mind is stayed on thee: because he trusteth in thee. Trust ye in the Lord for ever: for in the Lord Jehovah is everlasting strength." Verse 3 assures us of God's peace and verse 4 assures us of His strength. The phrase "the Lord Jehovah is everlasting strength" is literally, "the Lord Jehovah is the rock of ages." Every believer is standing on a solid foundation.

The Word of God provides comfort when it says, "Cast thy burden upon the Lord, and he shall sustain thee: he shall never suffer the righteous to be moved" (Ps. 55:22). Reminding yourself of promises like these will renew your confidence in God. You will also be encouraged as you see how others have trusted the Lord in times of adversity. Remember Job who said, "Though he slay me, yet will I trust in him" (13:15). Job's unshakable confidence in God will encourage you to have the same confidence.

Your confidence in God will be renewed as you see that He has promised victory over circumstances. Isaiah 43:2 records His promise that "when thou passeth through the waters, I will be with thee; and through the rivers, they shall not overflow thee: when thou walkest through the fire, thou shalt not be burned; neither shall the flame kindle upon thee." Remind yourself of this verse as you pass through the waters of sorrow, the rivers of danger, and the fires of testing. It will renew your confidence in God.

Pray

After you have renewed your confidence in God and have established yourself in Him, you should pray earnestly, definitely and believingly. Luke 18:1 says that "men ought always to pray, and not to faint." Psalm 50:15 records God's promise: "Call upon me in the day of trouble: I will deliver thee, and thou shalt glorify me." God delivers us in the sense that He enables us to stand up under our testings. We also see the power of prayer and the goodness of the Lord in Psalm 34:4-9: "I sought the Lord, and he heard me, and delivered me from all my fears. They looked unto him, and were lightened: and their faces were not ashamed. This poor man cried, and the Lord heard him, and saved him out of all his troubles. The angel of the Lord encampeth round about them that fear him, and delivereth them. O taste and see that the Lord is good: blessed is the man that

116

trusteth in him. O fear the Lord, ye his saints: for there is no want to them that fear him." Trust the Lord. Place your confidence in Him and you will find His grace sufficient for your every need.

Count Your Blessings

Another practical suggestion concerning suffering is to count your blessings. For the Christian, suffering ends in blessing. When your eyes are fixed on the blessing instead of the suffering, you will find great encouragement. One of the blessings that results from suffering is the power of endurance. This truth is emphasized in James 1:2-4: "Reckon it nothing but joy, my brethren, whenever you find yourselves surrounded by various temptations. Be assured that the testing of your faith leads to power of endurance; Only let endurance do its full work, so that you may become perfect and complete, deficient in nothing" (*Weymouth*).

The Scriptures also tell us that trials or tribulations work patience. Paul said, "We glory in tribulations also: knowing that tribulation worketh patience" (Rom. 5:3). When you adopt the same attitude that the Apostle Paul had you will find much strength in the midst of suffering. Tribulation works patience "and patience, experience; and experience, hope: And hope maketh not ashamed; because the love of God is shed abroad in our hearts by the Holy Ghost which is given unto us" (vv. 4,5). Are these things realities in your life? This is the purpose of suffering. These qualities are the blessings which result from suffering.

117

The Psalms record many blessings that are found in affliction. The psalmist said, "Before I was afflicted I went astray: but now have I kept thy word" (119:67). He then counts his blessings by saying, "It is good for me that I have been afflicted; that I might learn thy statutes" (v. 71). In verse 75 the psalmist said, "I know, O Lord, that thy judgments are right, and that thou in faithfulness hast afflicted me." The psalmist saw the purpose of affliction. His own experience taught him that the judgments of the Lord are right. You also will find this true as you take time in the Word of God to see all the blessings you have as a result of suffering.

The Book of Job also tells us of the blessings which result from suffering. Eliphaz said, "Behold, happy is the man whom God correcteth: therefore despise not thou the chastening of the Almighty: For he maketh sore, and bindeth up: he woundeth, and his hands make whole" (5:17,18). Notice the twofold action: God permits suffering but He binds up and makes whole again. No wonder Job could say, "When he hath tried me, I shall come forth as gold" (23:10).

Saturate Yourself With the Word

Another thing you need to do in the midst of suffering is to saturate your mind and heart with the Word of God. The psalmist realized the importance of being saturated with the Word of God, for he said, "Remember the word unto thy servant, upon which thou hast caused me to hope. This is my comfort and my affliction: for thy word hath quickened me" (119:49,50). In other words, the psalmist went to the Word of God and it encouraged him and gave him new life.

We who know the Lord Jesus Christ are like sheep following a shepherd. When the shepherd is in the presence of the sheep there is no other want. The psalmist referred to this by saying, "The Lord is my shepherd; I shall not want" (23:1). The entire Twenty-Third Psalm emphasizes that the Shepherd is in the midst of the sheep at all times. This is verified by the Lord's promise in the New Testament: "I will never leave thee, nor forsake thee" (Heb. 13:5).

Because the Lord will never leave or forsake the Christian, "we may boldly say, The Lord is my helper, and I will not fear what man shall do unto me" (Heb. 13:6). When you are confident that the Lord is at your side you will not fear men.

Perhaps you say, In my trials I have cried and cried to God, but He will not answer me. However, on the basis of Hebrews 13:5,6 you may be assured that Christ is there and He knows completely what you are going through. His heart is pained with the suffering He has to allow you, but He knows what the end product will be; therefore, He knows it is worth it all. You and I do not know, but He knows.

The Psalms also emphasize that since the Lord is with us we need not fear men. The psalmist said, "In God I will praise his word, in God I have put my trust; I will not fear what flesh can do unto me" (56:4). The psalmist concludes this psalm by saying, "For thou hast delivered my soul from death: wilt not thou deliver my feet from falling, that I may walk before God in the light of the living?" (v. 13). Because the Lord has saved us from hell, it is only normal to expect that the Lord will keep us from failing in this life if we depend on Him. We want to be an example to the people before whom we walk, so we need to depend on the Lord to keep us from failing.

Praise the Lord

Another suggestion concerning suffering is to practice praising the Lord when you are in the dark about suffering. But you say it is so hard to do that. That is true, but try it. Remember Paul and Silas who were put in prison after they had been beaten. Their backs were no doubt so sore they could not even lie down—plus their feet were placed in stocks. Yet we are told that at midnight they were praising God and singing hymns (Acts 16:25). They praised the Lord even though they were suffering. What was the result? A great earthquake shook the foundations of the prison which opened the doors of the prison and freed every prisoner from his bonds. Even though the prisoners could have run away, apparently they were so attracted by what they saw in Paul and Silas that they had no desire to leave. They wanted to find out more about the God of Paul and Silas. This teaches us that God has a purpose in our suffering so we should praise Him even though we may not understand His purpose. Paul and Silas experienced what Job described when he said that God is one "who giveth songs in the night" (35:10). We too can experience the same thing even in the midst of suffering.

Every Christian is commanded to "rejoice evermore. Pray without ceasing" (I Thess. 5:16,17). In other words, every time something
120

comes up we need to pray about it. It does not mean that we are constantly talking or speaking in prayer, but rather that we are praying incessantly about things which arise. The next verse commands: "In every thing give thanks: for this is the will of God in Christ Jesus concerning you." The "every thing" of this verse also includes affliction or suffering. We can give thanks to God even for suffering because we realize He is faithful and is accomplishing His purpose in our lives.

Forget Yourself; Love Others

In the midst of suffering, it will be especially helpful if you forget yourself and love and care for others. In Galatians 6:2 we are told, "Bear ye one another's burdens, and so fulfil the law of Christ." This we are to do while rejoicing in the Lord. Romans 12:15 emphasizes how we ought to identify ourselves with others: "Rejoice with them that do rejoice, and weep with them that weep." In other words, forget yourself and turn to others. We need to love others and encourage them in their trials. This is one of the reasons that God sends suffering to us—that we might be able to comfort others. In II Corinthians 1:4,5 God is described as the one "who comforteth us in all our tribulation, that we may be able to comfort them which are in any trouble, by the comfort wherewith we ourselves are comforted of God. For as the sufferings of Christ abound in us, so our consolation also aboundeth by Christ."

Submit Yourself to God

In our suffering we must always submit ourselves totally to God for a life of victory. By inspiration the Apostle Paul spoke to all Christians when he said, "I beseech you therefore, brethren, by the mercies of God, that ye present your bodies a living sacrifice, holy, acceptable unto God, which is your reasonable service" (Rom. 12:1). God wants us to be living sacrifices for Him. No matter how much we suffer, God will make a way of escape that we may be able to bear it. As we see the love of God in all of this, we can exclaim with the Apostle Paul, "Who shall separate us from the love of Christ?" (Rom. 8:35). Christ loves us so much that nothing is able to separate us from His love—not tribulation, distress, persecution, famine, nakedness, peril or sword. "In all these things we are more than conquerors through him that loved us" (v. 37). You can believe Christ and trust Him for everything. Nothing will ever be able to separate you from His love. He will not forget you in your suffering or permit you to suffer beyond what you are able to bear. Always remember that God's love for us is outgoing—from Him to us. Submit to Him and say, "Thank You, Lord. I know You are doing this for me and I am waiting upon You to see me through to victory." Be confident that "God is able to make all grace abound toward you; that ye, always having all sufficiency in all things, may abound to every good work" (II Cor. 9:8).

Thought: Distress is a blessing in disguise if it drives us to the power of faith and prayer.

Chapter 11

Suffering and the
Glory That Follows

Suffering and glory go hand in hand. Of at least 18 passages in the New Testament which refer to the suffering of the Lord Jesus Christ, 15 also refer to the glory that follows. In other words, almost every passage that mentions His suffering also refers to the result of the suffering—glory. It is also true for us that there will be glory on the other side of our suffering. Therefore we must look beyond our temporal suffering unto the eternal rewards.

Christ Anticipated the Glory to Follow

All during His suffering, the Lord Jesus Christ anticipated the glory that was to follow. John 12:23 records the words of Jesus who said, "The hour is come, that the Son of man should be glorified." At first it might seem that He was referring to His resurrection but the following verse shows this is not true. Jesus continued, "Except a corn of wheat fall into the ground and die, it abideth alone: but if it die, it bringeth forth much fruit." Jesus was talking about the fact that He was going to die. Yet He called this time the hour of

His glorification. He could do this because His eyes were fixed on the future—beyond the suffering, beyond the cross, beyond death. When Jesus was talking to the Heavenly Father, as recorded in chapter 17 of John, He "lifted up his eyes to heaven, and said, Father, the hour is come; glorify thy Son, that thy Son also may glorify thee" (v. 1). Here again He referred to "the hour." What hour? The time when He would be crucified. The suffering itself was not glorious but what He accomplished glorified the Father and also brought glory to Him, the Son. We too must look beyond the suffering to the glory that follows.

In Luke 24:26 we are told, "Ought not Christ to have suffered these things, and to enter into his glory?" How did Christ enter into His glory? By the things which He suffered. Hebrews 2:9 says, "But we see Jesus, who was made a little lower than the angels for the suffering of death, crowned with glory and honour; that he by the grace of God should taste death for every man." He was crowned with glory and honor, but mankind did not see the crown. The author of Hebrews—most likely the Apostle Paul—was referring to the glory that followed the suffering and death of the Lord Jesus Christ. Suffering and glory are thus brought together.

Suffering and glory are also seen together at the transfiguration. Peter, James and John witnessed Christ's transfiguration and saw Moses and Elijah talking with Christ. It is said that they "appeared in glory, and spake of his decease which he should accomplish at Jerusalem" (Luke 9:31). When Peter and those that were with him awoke they saw the glory of Christ and the two men that

124

were with Him. Appearing in His glory, Christ was giving Peter, James and John a glimpse of the future. Notice, however, that they did not tell others about it. Verse 36 tells us that "they kept it close, and told no man in those days any of those things which they had seen." Before the resurrection no one would be able to understand the significance of what the disciples had seen. After the resurrection, when Jesus Christ was glorified, they would begin to understand the true significance. Glory followed suffering for the Lord Jesus Christ.

Hebrews 12:2 emphasizes the glory that was beyond the suffering when it urges us to look to Jesus who is the "author and finisher of our faith; who for the joy that was set before him endured the cross, despising the shame, and is set down at the right hand of the throne of God." Christ saw the joy beyond the suffering. Because of the joy that was beyond the cross He was willing to endure the pain and shame. Thus we see that Jesus Christ is our example in suffering—He fixed His eyes on the glory that was beyond the suffering. Today this same Christ lives in those of us who have received Him as Saviour. Why does He indwell us? In order to produce the same kind of results in our lives. So while we are enduring affliction we need to keep our eyes fixed on the glory to follow. Our suffering will seem small and insignificant as we compare it to the glory that is to follow. God permits suffering at the present because He wants us to have many rewards and much glory in the future.

Suffering and glory are also placed together in Philippians 2:5-11 which tells us of Christ's humbling Himself and dying on the cross, then

125

being exalted above every name. It is emphasized that Christ is our example in this for we are told, "Let this mind be in you, which was also in Christ Jesus" (v. 5). How do we get His mind? By allowing Him who indwells us to control our lives completely. We need to say to Him, "Lord, You control my mind. I know You are living within me and I will accept Your way of thinking." As we submit ourselves to Christ in this manner we will have a completely different attitude.

After telling of Christ's humiliation and death on the cross, the Scriptures say, "Wherefore God also hath highly exalted him, and given him a name which is above every name: That at the name of Jesus every knee should bow, of things in heaven, and things in earth, and things under the earth; And that every tongue should confess that Jesus Christ is Lord, to the glory of God the Father" (Phil. 2:9-11). The "wherefore" of verse 9 connects the suffering of the Lord Jesus with the glory that followed. He is now seated above every principality and power. Ephesians 2:6 says that God "hath raised us up together, and made us sit together in heavenly places in Christ Jesus." This verse clearly sets forth the position that every believer has in Christ. Are you enjoying the glory with Christ or are you murmuring and complaining about the suffering of the present time?

In connection with the glory of Christ that followed His suffering, notice what Revelation 5:11,12 tells us. Here the Apostle John said, "And I beheld, and I heard the voice of many angels round about the throne and the beasts and the elders: and the number of them was ten thousand times ten thousand, and thousands of thousands;

Saying with a loud voice, Worthy is the Lamb that was slain to receive power, and riches, and wisdom, and strength, and honour, and glory, and blessing." What a majestic scene! Why is Jesus Christ worthy to receive power, riches, wisdom, strength, honor, glory and blessing? Because He suffered and was slain. John then tells us about the adoration of all of heaven for the Lord Jesus Christ: "And every creature which is in heaven, and on the earth, and under the earth, and such as are in the sea, and all that are in them, heard I saying, Blessing, and honour, and glory, and power, be unto him that sitteth upon the throne, and unto the Lamb for ever and ever" (v. 13).

Evaluate Your Afflictions and Yield to God

Evaluate your afflictions, therefore, and yield yourself to God to work out His purpose in you so that you might experience the glory to follow. Christ is our example in this, and He now indwells every believer to bring about victory through suffering so that all might experience the glory to follow. There is also a "wherefore" as far as our suffering is concerned. Because of our suffering there will be much glory to follow. Therefore, let us accept our suffering as from the Lord and begin to thank Him for what He is doing in and for us.

The Apostle Paul said, "For our light affliction, which is but for a moment, worketh for us a far more exceeding and eternal weight of glory" (II Cor. 4:17). Notice that our affliction works for us—isn't that a wonderful truth? The same thing is emphasized in Romans 8:17,18: "And if children, then heirs; heirs of God, and joint-heirs with Christ; if so be that we suffer with him, that we may be also glorified together. For I reckon that the sufferings of this present time are not worthy to be compared with the glory which shall be revealed in us."

Suffering in the will of God is our passport into an assured glory. We must learn to look at the trials of time in the light of eternity. We must contrast the present condition with our future state. Here it is affliction but there it will be glory. It is brief affliction in contrast to eternal glory. The present influences the future because the present afflictions prepare us for future glory.

Affliction draws our hearts away from the love of the world and makes us long for the time when we will be translated from this wicked world to the glory that follows. One day in the Father's house will be more than necessary to compensate for all the years that we have spent in suffering on earth. This causes suffering to lose its sting for we realize the more we suffer, the greater will be our abundant entrance into heaven. So we can write Romans 8:28 over every sorrow, trial or disappointment, realizing that God has chosen it as a means to bring glory to us by conforming us to the image of His Son.

As we consider the glory that follows suffering, we should also remember I John 3:2: "Beloved, now are we the sons of God, and it doth not yet appear what we shall be: but we know that, when he shall appear, we shall be like him; for we shall see him as he is." We must keep our eyes on this goal—to someday be like Jesus Christ. When we have this goal always before us then the following verse will also be true in our lives: "And every man that hath this hope in him purifieth himself, even as he is pure."

Wherefore

In the light of the glory that will follow suffering, we can say with the writer of Hebrews: "Wherefore lift up the hands which hang down, and the feeble knees" (12:12). In other words, get a grip on your heart. Let the Lord Jesus Christ really work in and through your life.

Peter put it another way when he wrote: "Wherefore gird up the loins of your mind, be sober, and hope to the end for the grace that is to be brought unto you at the revelation of Jesus Christ" (I Pet. 1:13). We gird up the loins of our minds as we get our goal in clear perspective and set our hearts on it. Notice that Peter emphasized the importance of the mind. Jesus Christ can control our minds if we turn them over to Him. The result will be newfound joy. "Think about the future," Peter said. "Think about the glory that is to follow at the coming of the Lord Jesus Christ."

Paul spoke much of the glory which followed suffering. Writing from a deep, dark dungeon in Rome, Paul looked into the future and wrote to Timothy: "For I am now ready to be offered, and the time of my departure is at hand. I have fought a good fight, I have finished my course, I have kept the faith" (II Tim. 4:6,7). Because Paul had suffered so much for the Lord Jesus Christ he could also say, "Henceforth there is laid up for me a crown of righteousness, which the Lord, the righteous judge, shall give me at that day: and not to me only, but unto all them also that love his appearing" (v. 8). Do you have a longing heart as you look forward to the Lord's appearance? Are you keeping uppermost in your mind the fact that Jesus Christ will someday soon return for His own?

In the last years of my father's abode on earth, he would so often say to me, "Son, I am looking for the uppertaker." My father was suffering considerably—physically and in many other ways—and he was anticipating with joy the time when he would meet his Lord and Saviour and experience the glory that was to follow.

The Scriptures make it clear that the glory which follows is contingent upon the suffering of this present time. Second Timothy 2:12 says, "If we suffer, we shall also reign with him: if we deny him, he also will deny us." This verse does not refer to salvation but to suffering in the right attitude. The way we deny Christ in our suffering is by murmuring, quarreling and questioning the things that the Lord is allowing to take place in our lives. If we deny Him in this way then He will deny us the privileges that are to come.

Romans 8:17 also emphasizes that the glory to follow depends on present suffering. This verse speaks to all Christians when it says, "And if children, then heirs; heirs of God, and joint-heirs with Christ; if so be that we suffer with him, that we may be also glorified together."

The same truth is also emphasized in Revelation 3:21: "To him that overcometh will I grant to sit with me in my throne, even as I also overcame, and am set down with my Father in his throne." How do we overcome? First, by receiving Christ as Saviour. First John 5:5 tells us, "Who is he that overcometh the world, but he that believeth that Jesus is the Son of God?" We also overcome in our Christian lives as we walk in dependence on the Lord and let Him live out His life through us. As we appropriate His strength to bear up under the trials, we become "more than conquerors through him that loved us" (Rom. 8:37). Christ overcame by keeping His eyes fixed on the joy that was set before Him. Because He knew of the glory to follow He was willing to endure the shame and pain of the cross.

The Spirit of Anticipation

We do not know all that is involved in the glory that follows suffering, but we need to let the Holy Spirit create in us the spirit of anticipation. The Apostle Paul's spirit of anticipation is seen in Philippians 3:10,11: "That I may know him, and the power of his resurrection, and the fellowship of his sufferings, being made conformable unto his death; If by any means I might attain unto the resurrection of the dead." When we carefully examine these verses we see that the Apostle Paul wanted to suffer with Christ so he could be made conformable to His life—Christ's resurrection life here and the glory that followed. Paul was looking into the future and was concentrating on the results that come from suffering when we suffer with the right attitude.

We have been made partakers with Christ in His death in the sense that when we received Christ as Saviour, we died to sin. Sin no longer has control over us for we are now free to live for Christ. Therefore, you are now to "reckon ye also yourselves to be dead indeed unto sin, but alive unto God through Jesus Christ our Lord" (Rom. 6:11). We experience glory in this life as we reckon

131

ourselves to be dead to sin but living unto God through Jesus Christ.

God's Anticipation

Not only do Christians have something to anticipate but there is an anticipation for God also. We see this anticipation in Psalm 116:15: "Precious in the sight of the Lord is the death of his saints." How is it possible to say that the death of saints is precious in the sight of the Lord? There are several reasons why this is so. First, the saints are precious to the Lord for they are the Father's love gift to Jesus Christ. We have been bought by the sufferings of Christ, and the Father rejoices when—after our suffering—He can present us to Jesus Christ as a love gift because of the way Jesus suffered. Saints are precious to the Lord because they are the results of the sufferings of Christ.

Second, the death of His saints is precious to the Lord because death terminates their sorrow and suffering. It is true that the Lord has allowed these sufferings and He could take them away, but then there would not be as much glory to follow. But even so the Lord is touched with the feelings of our infirmities and He rejoices when we are released from this life of suffering.

Third, death affords the Lord an opportunity to display His sufficiency. God has supplied our every need and at death the Lord has opportunity to reveal all that He has in store for His saints. We must take this by faith now but after death we will see these things face to face.

Fourth, the Lord rejoices in the death of His saints because at death they go directly to be with Him. Paul expressed this when he said, "We are confident, I say, and willing rather to be absent from the body, and to be present with the Lord" (II Cor. 5:8). The Christian who is absent from the body is present with the Lord. This truth is also seen in Philippians 1:23: "For I am in a strait betwixt two, having a desire to depart, and to be with Christ; which is far better." Here again we see that the believer goes directly into the presence of the Lord at death.

Jesus promised all believers that someday they would be in His presence. He said, "Let not your heart be troubled: ye believe in God, believe also in me. In my Father's house are many mansions: if it were not so, I would have told you. I go to prepare a place for you. And if I go and prepare a place for you, I will come again, and receive you unto myself; that where I am, there ye may be also" (John 14:1-3).

Jesus also said, "Father, I will that they also, whom thou hast given me, be with me where I am; that they may behold my glory, which thou hast given me: for thou lovedst me before the foundation of the world" (John 17:24). Jesus spoke these words while He was yet on earth, but He was anticipating the day when those who received Him as Saviour would be in His very presence. Christ's reason for wanting the saints to be in His presence was so "they may behold my glory, which thou hast given me." Christ wanted believers to share in His glory. Previous to this He had said, "The glory which thou gavest me I have given them; that they may be one, even as we are one" (v. 22). Although we have not yet seen this glory, it is positionally held in store for us. As mentioned in I Peter 1:4, it is "an inheritance

133

incorruptible, and undefiled, and that fadeth not away, reserved in heaven for you."

What a Wonderful Lord!

In all of this we see what a wonderful Lord we have. God has made a wonderful provision for us. We need to constantly remind ourselves of the words of Christ recorded in John 14:27: "Peace I leave with you, my peace I give unto you: not as the world giveth, give I unto you. Let not your heart be troubled, neither let it be afraid." Christ did not wait until a future time to give peace to His followers. You can experience the joy of His peace right now. He has arranged everything for us and is just waiting until that time when He can share His glory with us.

Jesus also told His disciples, "These things I have spoken unto you, that in me ye might have peace. In the world ye shall have tribulation: but be of good cheer; I have overcome the world" (John 16:33). While on earth, Jesus prayed to His Heavenly Father and said, "Holy Father, keep through thine own name those whom thou hast given me, that they may be one, as we are" (John 17:11). Even though believers would have to pass through tribulations and trials in this life, Christ wanted the Heavenly Father to keep them so that they might share in His glory after they had suffered. These are the provisions God has made for us.

It is only as we look unto Jesus that we will have the right attitude toward our suffering. In the booklet, *Looking Unto Jesus*, Theodore Monod says that we ought to be looking "unto Jesus and

134

not at our troubles, to count up their number, to reckon their weight, to find perhaps a certain strange satisfaction in tasting their bitterness. Apart from Jesus, trouble does not sanctify, it hardens or it crushes. It produces not patience, but rebellion; not sympathy, but selfishness; not hope (Rom. 5:3) but despair. It is only under the shadow of the cross that we can appreciate the true weight of our own cross, and accept it each day from His hand, to carry it with love, with gratitude, with joy; and find in it for ourselves and for others a source of blessings" (p. 11).

As we consider all that God wants to accomplish in and for us through suffering, and as we see the provisions He has made for us, we will exclaim with the Apostle Paul, "How fathomless the depths of God's resources, wisdom, and knowledge! How unsearchable His decisions, and how mysterious His methods! For who has ever understood the thoughts of the Lord, or has ever been His adviser? Or who has ever advanced God anything to have Him pay him back? For from Him everything comes, through Him everything lives, and for Him everything exists. Glory to Him forever! Amen" (Rom. 11:33-36, *Wms.*).

Thought: Great sufferers do the world's work; a crown of loftiest achievement is a crown of thorns.